I0221824

Anonymous

American Summer Resort and Country Board Directory

Anonymous

American Summer Resort and Country Board Directory

ISBN/EAN: 9783337037246

Printed in Europe, USA, Canada, Australia, Japan

Cover: Foto ©Andreas Hilbeck / pixelio.de

More available books at **www.hansebooks.com**

AMERICAN

Summer Resort and Country Board

DIRECTORY.

SEASON OF 1882.

OCEAN,

MOUNTAIN,

and FARM.

PUBLISHED BY

ALLEN & CO.,

5 Murray St., New York.

CONTENTS.

CONTENTS.—*Continued.*

PREFACE.

It has been our endeavor in preparing the **American Summer Resort Directory,** to meet the requirements of all classes who may have occasion to consult its pages. And if it does to any considerable extent fulfill this object, its mission will have been accomplished. Those who are limited as to time may find Sea Shore and Mountain Resorts brought within their reach, while those who have ample time and means will have the widest scope to select from. The places are confined to no particular section, but combine attractions from all parts of the country. The routes are arranged on several of the leading lines according to distance from New York City, to afford the most simple method for the conveniences of those consulting them.

To enable us to produce this work at a popular price, we have carefully excluded all surperfluous and unimportant matter, and adopted a rigid condensation of style, though no effort has been spared to make it as reliable as possible ; but in handling so many places some errors are liable to occur, and we would feel grateful to our readers for any corrections they may suggest.

U. S. MUTUAL ACCIDENT ASSOCIATION,

No. 409 BROADWAY, NEW YORK.

Before Mr. Sniffkins, the Broker, entered the Park, he thought the best bargain he ever made was the purchase of his handsome mare. When he left the Park he was of a different opinion. He said the contract he made with the UNITED STATES MUTUAL ACCIDENT ASSOCIATION to pay him $50 per week indemnity in case of being disabled and $10,000 in case of death by accident, at a cost of about $20 per annum, was, under existing circumstances, by all odds the better bargain. The policeman's report that he believed the mare could travel a mile in less than a minute causes Mr. Sniffkins no satisfaction. The Doctor thinks that with careful nursing his patient will be out in ten or twelve weeks.

Moral.—Insure in the United States Mutual Accident Association, 409 Broadway, New York.

$5,000 Insurance and $25 Weekly Indemnity secured at an annual cost of about $10, which is one-third the rate of stock companies.

$10,000 Insurance at corresponding rates.

All valid claims paid at sight.

CHAS. B. PEET, (of Rogers, Peet & Co.,) President.

JAS. R. PITCHER, Secretary.

NEW YORK AND PHILADELPHIA NEW LINE.

BOUND BROOK ROUTE

—FOR—

TRENTON AND PHILADELPHIA.

Passenger Station in New York, Central R. R. of N. J. Foot Liberty St.

QUICKEST TIME FROM CITY TO CITY,

Philadelphia to New York.

THROUGH IN 2 HOURS.

Double Track, Steel Rails, Stone Ballast, Hard Coal, Palace Cars.

STATIONS IN PHILADELPHIA.—Philadelphia and Reading R. R., 9th and Green Streets; 3d and Berks Streets; 9th and Columbia Avenue.

Direct connection to and from Germantown, Manayunk, Norristown, Conshohocken, &c.

Tickets for sale at foot of Liberty Street, New York, and at principal hotels and express offices in New York, and at railroad and steamboat ticket offices throughout New York and New England.

H. P. BALDWIN,
G. P. A. C. R. R. of N. J., New York.

C. G. HANCOCK,
G. P. & T. A. P. & R. R. R., Philadelphia.

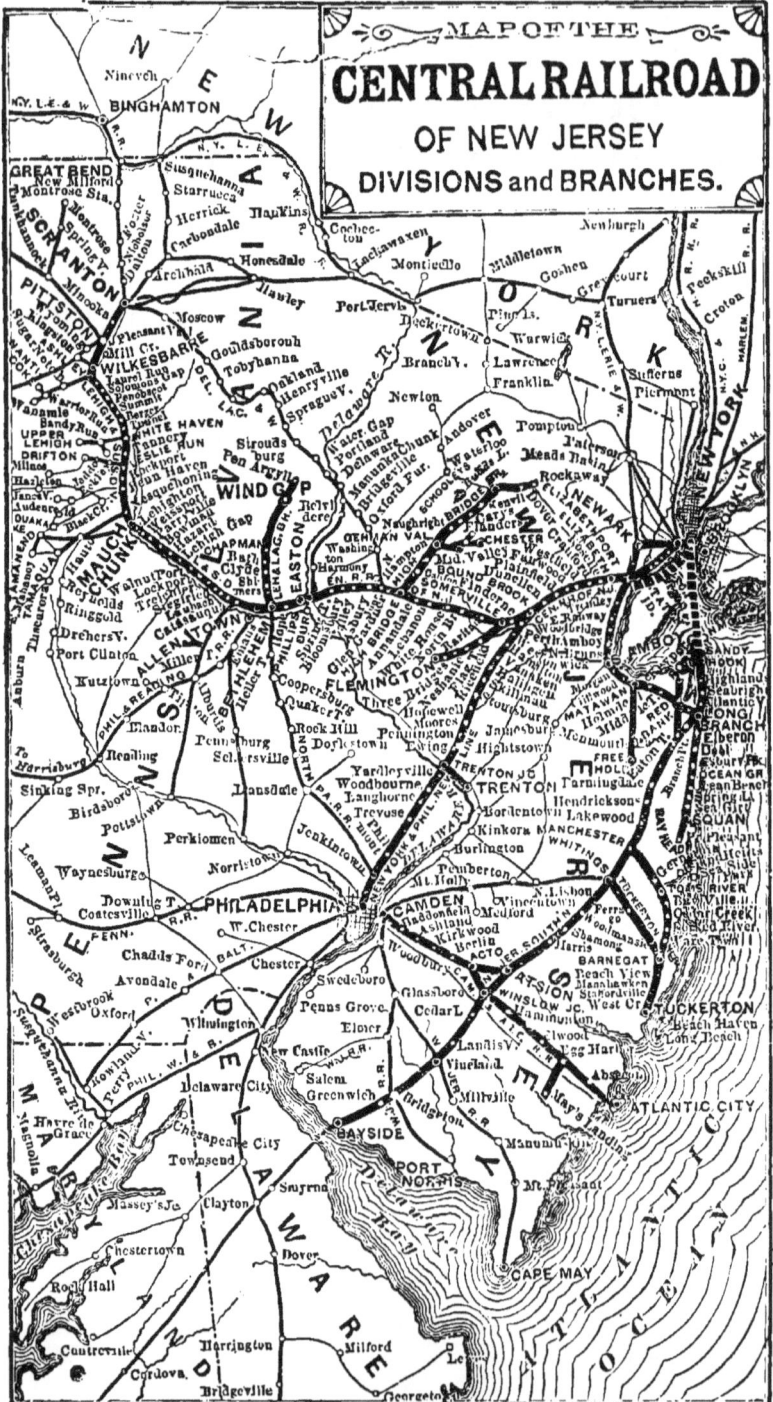

MAP OF THE
CENTRAL RAILROAD
OF NEW JERSEY
DIVISIONS and BRANCHES.

Central R. R. of New Jersey and Branches.

The region traversed by this road has indeed been most aptly described as the "Central Garden Spot" of New Jersey. Some of the richest farming lands in the Union pours its treasures into the metropolitan markets by this line. Vales and uplands, meadows and orchards, cozey hamlets and prosperous towns, and all the infinite variety of smiling landscapes confront the traveler everywhere along this perfect system. Its numerous branches afford direct access to the whole group of New Jersey coast resorts, from Sandy Hook to Atlantic City, to the mountain and lake regions of the same State and Pennsylvania to the Delaware Water Gap—its famous "Switzerland of America."

CENTRAL DIVISION.

BAYONNE, HUDSON CO., N. J.—7 miles from New York and only 22 minutes' ride. 28 trains daily.

Randall House accommodates, 40.............terms   to $10
Mrs. E. Paret, accommodates 10............... " $6 to   8

BERGEN POINT, HUDSON CO., N. J.—8 miles from New York, and situated at the intersection of Newark Bay and Kill Von Kull, and has long enjoyed a reputation for being a first class summer resort.

Latourette House, accommodates 500........terms $12 to $18
Beach Mansion, accommodates 30...........   "   12 to   15
Wykeman House, accommodates 100.......   "   5 to   10
Stringham House, accommodates 50........ ...   "   7 to   10
Ward Cottage, accommodates 15............   "   5 to   8
Van Buskirk Cottage, accommodates 25....   "   5 to   12
Bay Site, accommodates 17.................   "   8 to   12
Mrs Galt, accommodates 15.................   "   7 to   18

FANWOOD, SOMERSET CO., N. J.—21 miles from New York, and pleasantly located at the base of the Orange Mountains.

Brittin's House, accommodates 8............terms $8 to $12
Road House, accommodates 6..............   "   8 to   12
Mrs. Dunn, accommodates 5................   "   6 to   9
Mrs. Parse, accommodates 6................   "   7 to   10

PLAINFIELD, UNION CO., N. J.—24 miles from New York. A handsome city of 10,000 inhabitants, built on an elevated plain.

Park House, accommodates 125	terms $10	to	$25
G. Miller, accommodates 60	" 8	to	20
City Hotel, accommodates 75	" 8	to	25
Farmer's Hotel, accommodates 40	" 6	to	12
Somerset Hotel, accommodates 40	" 6	to	12
Box 548, accommodates 6	" 9	to	15

ANNANDALE, HUNTERTON CO., N. J.—51¼ miles from New York ; a pleasant and attractive village and celebrated for its milk and dairy farms.

Annandale House, accommodates 20	terms	$6
Clinton House, accommodates 25	"	6
Union House, accommodates 25	"	6

BETHLEHEM, HUNTERTON CO., N. J.—86 miles from New York, via Lehigh and Susquehanna Division. There is much picturesque scenery at this point. Above and around the island, the Lehigh rushes along, and with its open glades and green lawns, shaded by towering trees, combine to make it a chosen spot for summer boarders.

Sun Hotel, accommodates 175	terms $8	to	$12
Eagle Hotel, accommodates 175	" 8	to	12
American Hotel, accommodates 75	" 6	to	8

ALLENTOWN, LEHIGH CO., PA.—91 miles from N. Y., via Lehigh and Susquehanna Division. The scenery and natural curiosities at and near Allentown are well worth seeing. Among the objects of interest are: "Mammoth Rock;" elevation, 1,200 feet; "Worman's Springs," and "Helfrich's Cave."

American Hotel, accommodates 150	terms	$10
Allen House, accommodates 100	"	12
Eagle Hotel, accommodates 100	"	7
Cross Keys Hotel, accommodates 50	"	6
Black Bear Hotel, accommodates 50	"	5
Pennsylvania Hotel, accommodates 50	"	7
Centennial Hotel, accommodates 30	"	4

CATASAUQUA, LEHIGH CO., PA.—94 miles from N. Y., via Lehigh and Susquehanna Division. Pleasantly laid out on the Lehigh Canal and River.

Mansion House, accommodates 20	terms $5	to	$10
Eagle Hotel, accommodates 50	" 5	to	7
Pennsylvania Hotel, accommodates 50	" 5	to	7
Catasauqua House, accommodates 25	"		5
American House, accommodates 50	"		5

NEW JERSEY, SOUTHERN BRANCH.

By this route a regular and fast line of steamers will leave Pier 14, North River, foot of Liberty street, daily, passing through New York Bay, the Narrows, the Government Islands and Forts, and Staten Island to Sandy Hook, where trains are taken which closely follow the beach on a narrow neck of land. Shrewsbury River, on the right, and the Atlantic Ocean, on the left, to the Highlands of the Naversink, the summit of which commands a view of many miles of land and water. Highland village lies at the bottom of the heights, with the Naversink River flowing at its doors. From Highlands to Long Branch the entire coast is built up with handsome cottages, and seems like a continuous town.

HIGHLANDS, MONMOUTH CO., N. J.—24 miles from N. Y.
This is the highest point on the Atlantic coast; both still water and surf bathing may be enjoyed, and boating in every style.

East View House, accommodates 200 _____terms $10 to $12
Pavilion Hotel, accommodates 300 _____ "   10 to 16
Swift House, accommodates 80 _____ "   15 to 30
Highland Cottage, accommodates 100 _____ "   10 to 12

BELLEVUE, MONMOUTH CO., N. J.—25 miles from N. Y., and midway between the Highlands and Seabright.

Bellevue Hotel, accommodates 200 _____terms $21 to $28
Hotel Shrewsbury, accommodates 175 _____ "   21 to 28

SEABRIGHT, MONMOUTH CO., N. J.—26 miles from N. Y.
It is a pleasantly-located seaside town, on a narrow strip of beach, between the Shrewsbury River and the ocean.

Octagon House, accommodates 225 _____terms $20 to $25
Peninsula Hotel, accommodates 175 _____ "   15 to 20
Seabright Hotel, accommodates 75 _____ "   15 to 20

OCEANPORT, MONMOUTH CO., N. J.—34 miles from N. Y., and situated directly on the Shrewsbury River, and within a short distance of Monmouth Park Race Course.

Hendrick Smock, accommodates 20 _____ ____terms $8
Park Hotel, accommodates 40 _____ "   10
Riverside Cottage, accommodates 35 _____ " $8 to 10
Croxson House, accommodates 20 _____ "   8

LAKEWOOD, OCEAN CO., N. J.—36 miles from N. Y., and pleasantly located by a beautiful lake. Fine scenery and good drives.

Laurel House, accommodates 80 _____terms $21
Mansion House, accommodates 40 _____ " $10 to 12
Talmage House, accommodates 20 _____ "   6 to 8

TOMS RIVER, OCEAN CO., N. J.—68 miles from N. Y. An old and delightfully located town, and perfectly healthy. The bay and river affords excellent boating and fishing. Reached via N. J. Southern.

Magnolia House, accommodates 125........terms $10 to $16
Ocean House, accommodates 60............   "   10
Toms River Hotel, accommodates 50 ....   "   10

ISLAND HEIGHTS, OCEAN CO., N. J.—2 miles from Tom's River Station, and fronting on Tom's River and Barnegat Bay. It is a favorite Methodist Camp Meeting ground.

Island House, accommodates 125...........terms $6 to $10
Lawrence House, accommodates 30.........   "   8 to   12

KNEVIL, MORRIS CO., N. J.—Reached via the High Bridge branch of the C. R. R. of N. J. One of the most delightful spots in the State surrounded by lakes and mountains.

Succasunna House, accommodates 100...........terms $15
Vanatta House, accommodates 40.............   "   12
Roxbury House, accommodates 50.............   "   8
Drakeville House. accommodates 30.............   "   8
Lakeview House, accommodates 300.............   "   15
W. Sheer, accommodates 50...................   "   7
O. Van Every, accommodates 50...............   "   12

BEACH HAVEN, OCEAN CO., N. J.—A sea-side resort having few equals, and the best of surf-bathing, yachting and fishing. It is located on an island five miles from Tuckerton, and reached from that point by a small steamboat.

R. B. Engle accommodates 300...........terms $12 to $16
Parry House, accommodates 250...........   "   12 to   16
Beach Haven House, accommodates 100....   "   8 to 12
Ocean House, accommodates 50...........   "   8 to 12

FORKED RIVER, OCEAN CO., N. J.—76 miles from N. Y. No town on the coast has finer facilities for fishing, boating and bathing. The Weak-fish grounds of Barnegat Bay are in close proximity.

Lafayette House accommodates 75.........terms $12
Riverside House, accommodates 75........   " $9 to 12

BARNEGAT, OCEAN CO., N. J.—88 miles from N. Y.; convenient to Barnegat Bay. Its attractions are of the highest order to summer visitors for excellent sea bathing, and is famous for its fishing and great abundance of wild fowl.

Clarence House, accommodates 50.............terms $7
Floating House, accommodates 50...............   "   8
Mullen House, accommodates 30...............   "   7
J. S. Jennings, accommodates 100...............   " apply.
Club House, accommodates 25...............   "   "

ATLANTIC CITY, ATLANTIC CO., N. J.—126 miles from N. Y. This is one of the most celebrated summer resorts on the New Jersey coast. The houses are mostly built on an island just off from the mainland, called Absecom Beach. The island is ten miles long. The bathing beach is one of the best on the coast. Atlantic City also enjoys a high reputation as a health resort, being visited all the year round by invalids from all parts of the country.

	per week.
United States Hotel, accommodates......terms	$15 to $21
Brighton Hotel	" 15 to 25
Sea Side Hotel	" 15 to 25
Hadden House	" 12 to 20
Albion Hotel	" 12 to 20
Congress Hall	" 14 to 21
Ocean Hotel	" 15 to 20
Colonade Hotel	" 14 to 18
Mansion House	" 12 to 18
Clarendon Hotel	" 14 to 18
Brunswick Hotel	" 14 to 18
Park Avenue Hotel	" 12 to 18
Westminster Hotel	" 12 to 18
Ocean View Hotel	" 12 to 18
Stockton Hotel	" — —
Glendale Hotel	" 10 to 16
Arlington Hotel	" 12 to 18
La Pierre Hotel	" 12 to 18
Mary Hotel	" 12 to 18
Central Hotel	" 12 to 16
Fifth Avenue Hotel	" 12 to 16
Metropolitan Hotel	" 14 to 18
Delevan House	" 12 to 18
Beaumont Hotel	" 10 to 16

BRIDGETON, CUMBERLAND CO., N. J.—127 miles from N. Y.

Davis House, accommodates 75............terms	$5 to $10
City Hotel, accommodates 40	" 5 to 10
West Jersey Hotel, accommodates 25	" 5 to 8
Mrs. Crouse, accommodates 15	" 5
Mr. Fithian, accommodates 20	" 5

NEW YORK AND LONG BRANCH DIVISION.

This branch of the Central Railroad of New Jersey has done more for the development of the rich and inviting shore counties of the State than all other roads combined. It brings the metropolis and the popular resorts and population of the coast into the closest and most intimate relationship. Ultimately, no doubt the facilities which this line of communications affords will result in the establishment of a continuous line of towns with a permanent population from Sandy Hook to Barnegat. By this route is reached Long Branch, Ocean Grove, Sea Girt, Point Pleasant and intermediate stations, and to stations on the New Jersey Southern Railroad.

PERTH AMBOY, MIDDLESEX CO., N. J.—22 miles from N. Y.
It is situated on Raritan Bay at the mouth of the Raritan River.

Parker House, accommodates 40	terms	$7
Park House, acommodates 30	"	6
Pennsylvania House, accommodates 30	"	6
Eaglewood Park House, accommodates 100	"	10
Mrs. J. Thompson, accommodates 18	"	6
Geo Tice, accommodates 10	"	5

MATTAWAN, MONMOUTH CO., N. J.—29 miles from N. Y.
This place has many attractions for summer boarders, good walks and drives.

Mattawan House, accommodates 75	terms	$10
Mount Pleasant House, accommodates 40	"	7

KEYPORT, MONMOUTH CO., N. J.—2 miles from Mattawan station, on the Long Branch Division, or may be reached by boat direct from N. Y. It is pleasantly situated on Raritan Bay, which affords good boating and fishing.

J. D. Sickles, accommodates 100	terms	$7	to	$10
N. Johnson, accommodates 50	"	7	to	10
C. & D. B. Walling, accommodates 60	"	7	to	10
J. D. Hopkins, accommodates 60	"	7	to	10
W. Hornby, accommodates 25	"	6	to	8
Jacob Decker, accommodates 5	"	5	to	6
Dobson House, accommodates 50	"	7	to	10
Hilton House, accommodates 40	"	7	to	10

RED BANK, MONMOUTH CO., N. J.—39 miles from N. Y. It pleasantly situated on the Naversink River. It is surrounded by beautiful drives. Good boating, fishing and bathing.

Globe Hotel, accommodates 150............terms	$10 to	$15
Central Hotel, accommodates 50............. "	8 to	10
Union Hotel, accommodates 50.............. "	8 to	10
Prospect Hotel, accommodates 200 .... "	10 to	15
Leighton Hotel accommodates 160 .... "	8 to	10
Riverside Hotel, accommodates 50 .... "	8 to	12
D. E. Forest Hotel, accommodates 50....... "	8 to	10
Champlain Hotel, accommodates 60......... "	8 to	10

LITTLE SILVER, MONMOUTH CO., N. J.—41 miles from N. Y. Pleasantly located for summer boarders, with every attraction including fishing, boating and crabbing.

Point View House, accommodates 50 ....terms		$10
Silver Bay House, accommodates 125........ "	$10 to	$12
Borden's Hotel, accommodates 100.......... "	10 to	12
Park Hotel, accommodates 50............... "		10
Mulliner's Cottage, accommodates 20........ "		10

BRANCHPORT, MONMOUTH CO., N. J.—44 miles from N. Y., and is the nearest station to Long Branch. It is at the head of Pleasure Bay, which affords many pleasures to summer visitors, and is also conveniently located to the ocean.

Branchport House, accommodates 150 ......terms	$10 to	$15
Long Branch Hotel, accommodates 200...... "	10 to	15
Newings Hotel, accommodates 125.......... "		10
Riverside House, accommodates 150 .... "		10
Price's Hotel, accommodates 100 .... "	5 to	10
Thompsons Hotel, accomodates 100 .... "	10 to	12

LONG BRANCH, MONMOUTH CO., N. J.—45 miles from N. Y., "right on" the ocean. This is one of the most popular of American summer resorts ; the drives in the vicinity are of a most excellent character, and the bathing cannot be surpassed anywhere along the coast. The hotels at this point are among the best in the world. Long Branch can also be reached by boats direct from New York.

West End Hotel, accommodates 1,500,terms per day		$4 to	$5
Howland House, accommodates 800 .	"	"	4 to 5
Jauch's Hotel, accommodates 300....	"	"	4
Atlantic Hotel, accommodates 350 ...	"	"	3 50
United States Hotel,accommodates 800	"	"	3 50
Mansion House, accommodates 650 ..	"	"	3 50
Ocean House, accommodates 1,200...	"	"	4 to 5
Ocean Wave, accommodates 300.....	"	"	3
Florence, accommodates 200	"	"	3
Hotel Brighton, accommodates 500...	"	"	4 to 5
Germania, accommodates 150........	"	"	2 50
Mrs. Hoe, accommodates 150........	"	"	2 50
Mrs. Stroke, accommodates 100	"	"	2 to 3
Abbotsford, accommodates			

ELBERON, MONMOUTH CO., N. J.—47 miles from New York, and pleasantly located, directly on the ocean.

Elberon Hotel, accommodates 200.............terms, Apply
Holley Hotel, accommodates 60.............   '' $10 to 13

DEAL BEACH, MONMOUTH CO., N. J.—49 miles from New York ; right on the ocean.

Allen House, accommodates 80.....................terms $14
Roselle Cottage, accommodates 36.................... ''   14
Robinson Cottage, accommodates 20................. ''   10
Hathaway House, accommodates 250................. ''   15

ASBURY PARK, MONMOUTH CO., N. J.—50 miles from New York ; fronting directly on the ocean for a distance of one mile. The beach at this point is very fine and safe for bathing, and abundant facilities are offered ; the hotel and private boarding accommodations are of the very best ; a cheap, well-regulated hack system has been established, and pleasant drives may be enjoyed for a small expense; directly south of Asbury Park is Ocean Grove, from which it is separated by Wesley Lake, a beautiful body of fresh water, nearly three-quarters of a mile in length.

Coleman House, accommodates 500..terms $3 to $4 per day.
Ocean House, accommodates 400 ....   ''   12 to 18 per week.
West End Hotel, accommodates 250..   ''   12 to 20   ''
Brunswick Hotel, accommodates 250.   ''
Colorunade Hotel, accommodates 250. ·'   12 to 18   ''
Oriental Hotel, accommodates 225...   ''   15 to 20   ''
Metropolitan Hotel, accommodates 225 ''   15 to 20   ''
Grand Avenue Hotel, accommodates
  200 ....   ''   10 to 15   ''
Sunset Hall, accommodates 200......   ''   10 to 15   ''
Surf House, accommodates 125......   ''   10 to 15   '
Bristol Hotel, accommodates 125 ....   ''   10 to 18
Gramercey Hotel, accommodates 100.   ''   10 to 15
North End Hotel, accommodates 100.   ''   12 to 15   '
Asbury Hotel, accommodates 100....   ''   8 to 15   '
Princeton Hotel, accommodates 95...   ''   10 to 15   '
Belvedere Hotel, accommodates 75...   ''   10 to 15   '
St. Albans Hotel, accommodates 75..   ''   15 to 21   '
Curlew Hotel, accommodates 75.....   ''   10 to 12   '
Lake View Hotel, accommodates 75..   ''   10   ''
Guy Mansion House, accommodates 70 ''   10 to 15   ''
St. Claire House, accommodates 70...   ''   10 to 14   ''
Richmond House, accommodates 65..   ''   10 to 15   ''
Crescent House, accommodates 60...   ''   10 to 12   ''
Belleview Hotel, accommodates 60...   ''   10 to 12   ''
Irving House, accommodates 60......   ''   10 to 15   ''
Renwick Hotel, accommodates 60....   ''   8 to 12   ''
Sea View Hotel, accommodates 60...   ''   8 to 12   ''
Trojan Hotel, accommodates 50 .....   ''   8 to 10   ''
Norwood Hotel, accommodates 50...   ''   10 to 15   ''
Nassau Hotel, accommodates 50.....   ''   10 to 15   ''

Gillette House, accommodates 50...terms $10 to 12 per week.

Star Cottage, accommodates 50	" 10 to 15	"
Elberon Cottage, accommodates 50	" 8 to 10	"
Lookout Cottage, accommodates 50	" 8 to 15	"
Orange Cottage, accommodates 50	" 8 to 15	"
New England Cottage, accommodates 50	" 10 to 15	"
The Franklin Cottage, accommodates 50	" 10 to 15	"
Stockton Cottage, accommodates 45	" 10	"
Silverdean Cottage, accommodates 40	" 10 to 12	"
Grand View Hotel, accommodates 40	" 12 to 14	"
Ferry Villa Hotel, accommodates 40	" 8 to 15	"
Ashland Cottage, accommodates 40	" 12 to 15	"
Central Cottage, accommodates 40	" 8 to 10	"
Sunset Lake Cottage, accommodates 40	" 10 to 15	"
Ten Broeck Cottage, accommodates 40	"	
Hope Cottage, accommodates 40	" 8 to 10	"
Tyler Cottage, accommodates 40	" 8 to 12	"
Kernwood Cottage, accommodates 40	" 10 to 12	"
Brighton Villa, accommodates 40	" 7 to 14	"
Waverley Cottage, accommodates 35	" 8 to 12	"
Trenton House, accommodates 35	" 10 to 12	"
Windsor Cottage, accommodates 35	" 10 to 12	"
Albertson Villa, accommodates 35	" 10 to 15	"
Park Cottage, accommodates 35	" 8 to 12	"
Anchorage House, accommodates 35	" 10 to 12	"
Fifth ave. Cottage, accommodates 30	" 8 to 10	"
Neptune Cottage, accommodates 30	" 8 to 10	"
Wright Cottage, accommodates 30	" 10 to 12	"
Wilson Cottage, accommodates 30	" 9 to 12	"
Villa De Horton, accommodates 30	" 10 to 12	"
East End Cottage, accommodates 30	" 10 to 12	"

OCEAN GROVE, MONMOUTH CO., N. J.—Directly south of Asbury Park, celebrated the world over as a popular resort for Methodists, and the seat of their great camp meetings. It possesses every attraction to be met with at the sea side, combined with those of fresh water lakes. Time from N. Y. one hour and thirty-eight minutes.

Sheldon House, accommodates 300	terms $10 to $20	
The Arlington House, accommodates 300	" 12 to 20	
Howland House, accommodates 150	" 10 to 12	
Atlantic Hotel, accommodates 150	" 10 to 20	
La Pierre House, accommodates 150	" 10 to 15	
Spray View House, accommodates	"	
Ocean Hotel, accommodates 125	" 10 to 18	
Centennial Hotel, accommodates 125	" 7 to 12	
Metropolitan Hotel, accommodates 125	" 10 to 15	
Work Woman's Hotel, accommodates 113	" 3	
Thorne Cottage, accommodates 100	" 10 to 15	
Surf Avenue Hotel, accommodates 100	" 8 to 15	
Sea Side Hotel, accommodates 100	" 12 to 16	

The Madison House, accommodates 100....terms	$10 to	$15
National Hotel, accommodates 100.......... "	12 to	15
Lake Shore Hotel, accommodates 85........ "	9 to	15
The Clarendon Hotel, accommodates 80.... "	8 to	12
The Waverley Hotel, accommodates 85.... "	8 to	12
Aldine Hotel, accommodates 75........... "	7 to	14
Grove Cottage, accommodates 70.......... "	8 to	12
Germantown Hotel, accommodates 65...... "	8 to	12
Ocean Queen Hotel, accommodates 60..... "	12 to	18
Season Hotel, accommodates 60........... "	10 to	15
Ocean View Hotel, accommodates 60...... "	8 to	12
Le Chevalier Hotel, accommodates 60...... "	9 to	12
Jackson Hotel, accommodates 60.......... "	8 to	12
Lawrence Hotel, accommodates 60........ "	8 to	10
Broadway Hotel, accommodates 60....... "		
Block House, accommodates 55.......... "		10
Pennsylvania Hotel, accommodates 50..... "	7 to	10
Linwood Hotel, accommodates 50......... "	7 to	15
Gem Cottage, accommodates 50.......... "	8 to	12
Mansion House, accommodates 50........ "	8 to	10
Taylor's Restaurant, accommodates 50..... "	8 to	10
Hayward Cottage, accommodates 40....... "	8 to	12
Elm Cottage, accommodates 40........... "	4 to	6
Grantic State Cottage, accommodates 40... "	8 to	12
Gillingham Cottage, accommodates 40..... "	7 to	9
Pearl Cottage, accommodates 40.......... "	7 to	12
Glenwood Cottage, accommodates 40...... "	7 to	10
Ocean Villa Cottage.................... "	9 to	12
Cowell House, accommodates 40.......... "	8 to	12
The Irvington Cottage, accommodates 40... "	10 to	15
Mulford Cottage, accommodates 40........ "	9 to	10
Ocean Front Cottage, accommodates 40.... "	8 to	12
Amherst Cottage, accommodates 40........ "	9 to	10
Manchester Cottage, accommodates 40..... "	8 to	12
Bath Avenue Cottage, accommodates 35.... "	8 to	10
Page Cottage, accommodates 30.......... "	8 to	10
Mt. Tabor, accommodates 30............. "	8 to	10
Chautauqua Cottage, accommodates 30.... "	10 to	15
Maryland Cottage, accommodates 30....... "	8 to	12
Ivy Cottage, accommodates 30........... "	6 to	10
Pitman Cottage, accommodates 30........ "	6 to	10
Boylston Cottage, accommodates 25....... "	8 to	12
Palace Cottage, accommodates 25......... "	8 to	10
Keystone Cottage, accommodates 25...... "		8
Highland Cottage, accommodates 20...... "	7 to	10
Alpine Cottage, accommodates 20......... "	8 to	12
Wyoming Cottage, accommodates 10...... "	8 to	10

OCEAN BEACH, MONMOUTH CO., N. J.—53 miles from New York, on Shark River and fronting directly on the ocean. Good bathing and fishing facilities.

Surf House, accommodates 150..........terms	$12 to	$15
Colorado House, accommodates 260........ "	14 to	18

Neptune House, accommodates 150.........terms		$18
Atlantic House, accommodates 100.......... "	$12 to	15
Fifth Avenue House, accommodates 50..... "	10 to	15
Brunswick, accommodates 65.............. "	10 to	15
Carleton Cottage, accommodates 50........ "	6 to	10
Crystal Cottage, accommodates 50......... "	12 to	15
Windsor House, accommodates 100........ "	10 to	15
Columbia House, accommodates 250........ "	15 to	24
Ocean Beach House, accommodates 50..... "	7 to	12
La Pierre House, accommodates 35......... "	10 to	15
Delaware House, accommodates 60........ "	12 to	15
Mansion House, accommodates 50......... "	8 to	12

SPRING LAKE, MONMOUTH CO., N. J.—54 miles from New York. Here may be found every attraction to be met with in boating, bathing and fishing, either in the lakes or ocean.

Monmouth House, accommodates 800.......terms		$24
Carleton House, accommodates 250.......... "		18
Allaire Hotel, accommodates 200.......... "	$16 to	30
Essex Hotel, accommodates 200........... "	16 to	30
Surf Cottages, accommodates 200.......... "	16 to	30
Lake House, accommodates 250........... "	12 to	24
Sea View Hotel, accommodates 100......... "	10 to	18
Villa Park Hotel, accommodates 45........ "		10
Ocean Hotel, accommodates 125...........terms		15
Palmer House, accommodates 80.... ...... "		12
Wensor Cottage, accommodates 70.......... "		12
Lake View Cottages, accommodates 70...... "	8 to	16
Glendale Cottage, accommodates 60........ "	8 to	12
Chaplin Cottages, accommodates 40........ "	8 to	12
Townsend Cottage, accommodates 70....... "		18

SEA GIRT, MONMOUTH CO., N. J.—57 miles from New York. It is a pleasant and well shaded sea-side town, fronting directly on the ocean.

Beach Hotel, accommodates 300...........terms	$12 to	$35
Parker House, accommodates 80........... "	10 to	25
Gregg House, accommodates 100.......... "	10 to	25
Ventuor Cottage, accommodate 50........ "	10 to	15

MANASQUAN, MONMOUTH CO., N. J.—58 miles from New York, and pleasantly situated on Squan River, one mile and a half from the ocean.

Osborne House, accommodates 50.........terms	$8 to	$15
Morris House, accommodates 50.......... "	10 to	15
Havens House, accommodates 25.......... "	8 to	15
Union House, accommodates 100.......... "	10 to	20
Sea View Cottage, accommodates 25....... "	8 to	10
Ocean House, accommodates 75.......... "	10 to	20

POINT PLEASANT, OCEAN CO., N. J.—59 miles from New York ; is on the shore of Manasquan River. Its facilities for boating, bathing and fishing cannot be excelled, and its harbor is considered on of the safest on the coast.

Resort House, accommodates 200	terms	$10 to	$25
Ocean House, accommodates 200	"	10 to	25
Arnold House, accommodates 80	"	10 to	15
Curtis House, accommodates 60	"	10 to	15
Eureka House, accommodates 50	"	10 to	15
Clark House, accommodates 30	"	10 to	15
Riverside House, accommodates 35	"	10 to	15
Osborne House, accommodates 30	"	10 to	15
Allen House, accommodates 40	"	10 to	15
Brown's House, accommodates 30	"	10 to	15

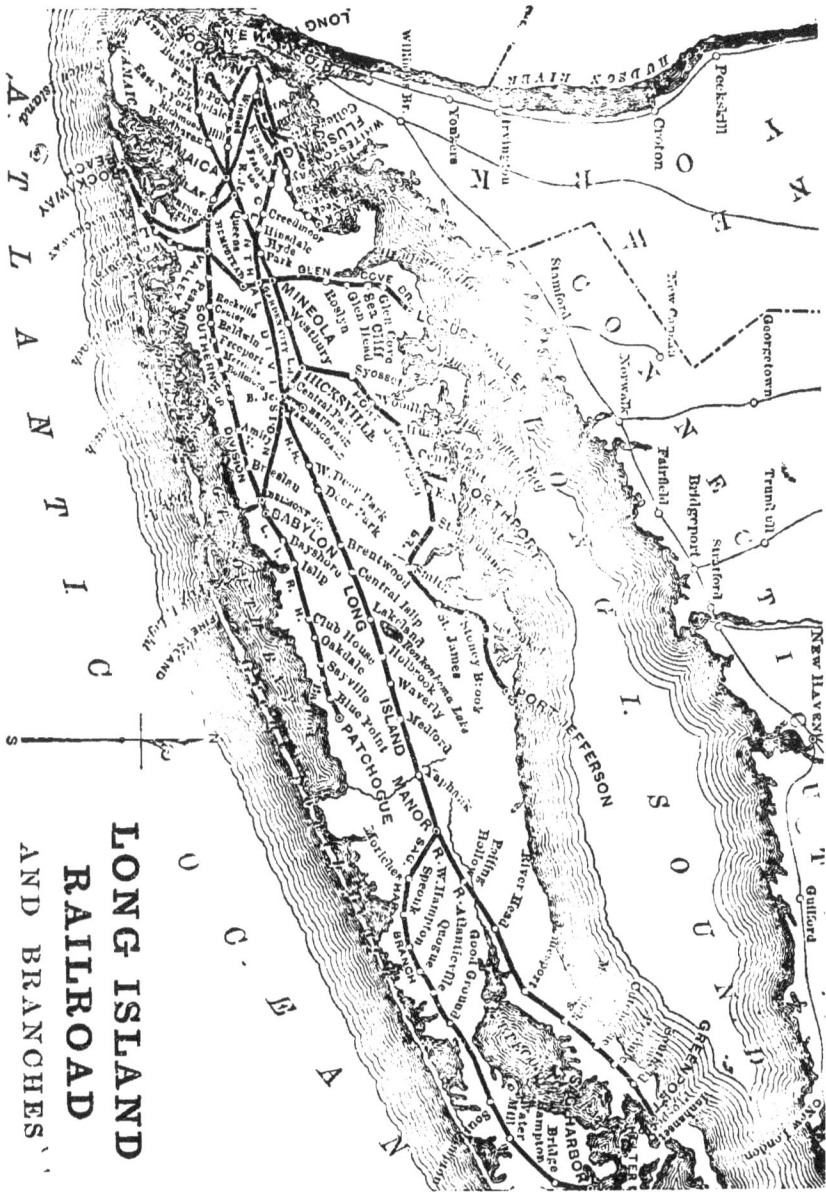

LONG ISLAND RAILROAD AND BRANCHES

LONG ISLAND R. R.

Much has been said and written about Long Island, and in preparing our DIRECTORY for this season, we have relied almost entirely on authority of this character for descriptions of localities, surroundings and real attractions, and considering that it has all emanated from or in the interest of the Long Island Railroad management, we promise our readers that another year we shall give them a most thorough and truthful description of the Island, and everything pertaining to it, not forgetting the Long Island Railway, its management, its equipment, and its service. We shall give in detail the exact distance of each station from the water where it is claimed boating, bathing, and fishing may be enjoyed. We will describe its shores and its approach, its facilities for bathing, the character of the water bed, the probabilities of catching fish, the facilities for boating, etc. We shall deal truthfully in the matter and speak of things as we find them. We shall unhesitatingly expose all malarious sections, and those addicted to insect pests. We shall give our readers the exact time from the City Hall, in New York, to each of the towns on the Island. We shall describe the drives, where there are any, and their character and the facilities for procuring conveyances. With this statement, we shall now proceed to give a list of parties on the Island who take summer boarders.

MONTAUK or SOUTHERN DIVISION.

There is a no more delightful, salubrious or generally attractive spot within a hundred miles of New York than along this section of the Long Island Railroad. Here you have all the advantages of forest, upland and open meadow, combined with the fresh salt air and cooling breezes from the bay and ocean. There are no better fishing grounds on the Atlantic coast, or safer boats, anywhere to be found, than abounds in the Great South Bay.

ROCKVILLE CENTRE, QUEENS CO., N. Y.—19 miles from
N. Y.; pleasantly located for summer boarding, and conveniently situated for boating, bathing, and fishing.

La Roza House, accommodates 30 _____ terms $6 to $8
Crossman House, accommodates 15 _____ " 6 to 8
Mrs. W. Wright, accommodates 12 _____ " 6 to 8
R. P. Chapin, accommodates 15 _____ " 5 to 6
Mrs. R. F. Soper. accommodates 12 _____ " 6 to 8

BALDWINS, QUEENS CO., N. Y.—21 miles from N. Y.; and
convenient to water where good boating, bathing and fishing can be had.

Baldwin House, accommodates 30 _____ terms $6 to $8
C. O. H. Craiggie, accommodates 20 _____ " 6 to 10
Mrs. S. Treadwell, accommodates 12 _____ " 5
Mrs. T. Baldwin, accommodates 12 _____ " 5

SOUTH OYSTER BAY, QUEENS CO., N. Y.—29 miles from N.
Y., on Great South Bay. Good drives, and fine boating, bathing and fishing.

Kilian's Hotel, accommodates 25 _____ terms $8 to $12
Vanderwater Hotel, accommodates 30 _____ " 8 to 12
Misses Vanderwater, accommodates 10 _____ " 8 to 12

AMITYVILLE, SUFFOLK CO., N. Y.—32 miles from N. Y.;
conveniently located near Great South Bay. Good boating,
bathing and fishing.

Southside House, accommodates 125 _____ terms $8 to $12
Revere House, accommodates 80 _____ " 8 to 12
Timothy Terry, accommodates 12 _____ " 7 to 10
Mrs. A. Birch, accommodates 12 _____ " 7 to 10
G. P. Williams, accommodates 30 _____ " 7 to 10
E. Wilmarth, accommodates 8 _____ " 7 to 10
Mrs. R. E. Seaman, accommodates 20 _____ " 7 to 10

BABYLON, SUFFOLK CO., N. Y.—37 miles from N. Y., and located directly on Great South Bay. Here are combined all
the attractions of the Island, with pure and bracing air at
all times. The fishing, boating and bathing cannot be surpassed. The drives are excellent, and surf-bathing is within
easy reach.

Watson House, accommodates 150 _____ terms $10 to $12
American House, accommodates 70 _____ " 10 to 12
Le Grange House, accommodates 70 _____ " 10 to 12
Washington Hotel, accommodates 30 _____ " 10 to 12
Mrs. T. S. Carll, accommodates 25 _____ " 8 to 12
Mrs. J. B. Cooper, accommodates 15 _____ " 8 to 10
Mrs. Eaton, accommodates 20 _____ " 8 to 10
Mrs. P. H. Hopkins, accommodates 12 _____ " 6 to 10
Mrs. P. Lumm, accommodates 25 _____ " 6 to 8

FIRE ISLAND, SUFFOLK CO., N. Y.—Located "out in the
Ocean." Take boat from Babylon. Time from N. Y., 2
hours.

Surf House accommodates 300 _____ terms $3 per day.

BAYSHORE, SUFFOLK CO., N. Y.—41 miles from N. Y. A well-known and popular resort convenient to the Bay and Ocean. Good drives, fine boating, bathing and fishing.

Dominy House accommodates 100..........terms		$15
Prospect House accommodates 150.......... "	$8 to	10
Howell House accommodates 35............ "	8 to	10
Mrs. Doxce, accommodates 15............. "	8 to	10
Theo. Coe, accommodates 10.... .... "		8

ISLIP, SUFFOLK CO., N. Y.—43 miles from N. Y. A well-known and favorite resort convenient to Ocean and Bay, where excellent boating, bathing and fishing can be had. the drives at this point are of the finest order.

Lake House accommodates 100 ....terms $12	to	$14
Pavilion Hotel accommodates 150............ "	9 to	12
Somerset House accommodates 20 .... "	8 to	12
H. S. Doxee, accommodates 12............. "	7 to	8
Mrs. A. Smith, accommodates 15............ "	6 to	8
Mrs. H. Whitman, accommodates 8........... "	6 to	8
Nelson Ketcham, accommodates 12.......... "	8 to	10

SAYVILLE, SUFFOLK CO., N. Y.—48 miles from N. Y. Located on Great South, where good boating, bathing and fishing may be had.

Bedell House accommodates 30...............terms $7	to	$10
Foster House accommodates 30............. "	7 to	10
I. C. Green, accommodates 25.............. "	7 to	10
Chas. G. Hulse,accommodates 25........... "	7 to	10
A. E. Hawkins, accommodates 20........... "	7 to	10
Dane House accommodates 30.............. "	7 to	10
W. G. Rogers, accommodates 12........... "	7 to	10

BAYPORT, SUFFOLK CO., N. Y.—51 miles from N. Y., in a delightful country situated on Great South Bay, where all the enjoyments of salt water may be realized.

Mrs. H. B. Palf, accommodates 15..........terms		$10
Mrs. W. Hooman, accommodates 12......... "	$7 to	8
Mrs. F. Edwards,accommodates 10.......... "	7 to	8
Mrs. Geo. Weeks, accommodates 10......... "	7 to	8
W. Needham, accommodates 28............ "	7 to	8
Garrett Smith, accommodates 10............ ".	7 to	8

BLUE POINT, SUFFOLK CO., N. Y.—53 miles from N. Y., and situated on Great South Bay. Every attraction is here offered, both on the land and bay. From this place come the celebrated Blue Point Oysters.

Joel Furman, accommodates 30..............terms $6	to	$10
W. Squires, accommodates 10 .... "	6 to	8
H. Bishop, accommodates 8 .... "	6 to	7
Mrs. H. Still, accommodates 10 .... "	6 to	8

PATCHOGUE, SUFFOLK CO., N. Y.—54 miles from N. Y., and directly on Great South Bay. A more favored spot for summer vacation could scarcely be found. Good boating bathing and fishing are among the attractions.

Roe's Hotel, accommodates 80 .... terms $8 to $10
Lewis Wicks, accommodates 25 ....   "   8 to 10
G. G. Horton, accommodates 25 ....   "   8 to 10
C. H. Willetts, accommodates 20 ....   "   8 to 10
Mrs. D. Baker, accommodates 10 ....   "   8 to 10
A. C. Mott, accommodates 10 ....   "   8 to 10

BELLPORT, SUFFOLK CO., N. Y.—58 miles from N. Y. Located directly on the Great South Bay. A pret y village abounding with every attraction for summer boarders. Excellent conveniences for surf and still water bathing.

Bellport, Bay House, accommodates 90 ...... terms $10 to $12
Mrs. M. Bell, accommodates 12 ....   "   8 to 10
Mrs. J. Shaw, accommodates 10 ....   "   8 to 10
Mrs. E. J. Raynor, accommodates 12 ....   "   8 to 10
Mrs. S Corwin, accommodates 15 ....   "   8 to 10
Mrs. N. Homan, accommodates 10 ....   "   8 to 10
Mrs. H. Terry, accommodates 10 ....   "   8 to 10
E. Post, accommodates 10 ....   "   8 to 10

CENTRE MORICHES, SUFFOLK CO., N. Y.—65 miles from N. Y., and located directly on Great South Bay. Fine boating and both surf and still-water bathing can be had almost at the door.

Long Island, accommodates 35 .... terms $7 to $10
Riverside House, accommodates 60 ....   "   8 to 10
Ketchum Hotel, accommodates 35 ....   "   7 to 10
William B. Howell, accommodates 30 ....   "   6 to 8
H. Robinson, accommodates 20 ....   "   6 to 8
E. P. Jarvis, accommodates 20 ....   "   6 to 8
Mrs. S. Terry, accommodates 20 ....   "   6 to 8
J. H. Bishop, accommodates 35 ....   "   6 to 8
A. Edwards, accommodates 25 ....   "   6 to 8
David Robinson, accommodates 20 ....   "   6 to 8
L. G. Terry, accommodates 20 ....   "   6 to 8
E Tapping, accommodates 20 ....   "   6 to 8

EAST MORICHES, SUFFOLK CO., N. Y.—67 miles from N. Y. Convenient to bay and ocean, which affords every degree of pleasure usually found at the sea shore.

D. F. Hulse, accommodates 15 .... terms $5 to $8
Wells Howard, accommodates 15 ....   "   5 to 8
J. Terry, accommodates 65 ....   "   5 to 8
H. F. Osborn, accommodates 25 ....   "   5 to 8
T. J. Tuthill, accommodates 60 ....   "   5 to 8
E. Howell, accommodates 10 ....   "   5 to 8
I. D. Gildersleeve, accommodates 10 ....   "   5 to 8
H. C. Smith, accommodates 30 ....   "   5 to 8
C. B. Elmore, accommodates 12 ....   "   5 to 8
A. W. Palmer, accommodates 15 ....   "   5 to 8
L. Pelletrau, accommodates 30 ....   "   5 to 8
John Robinson, accommodates 15 ....   "   5 to 8
Hiram Howell, accommodates 15 ....   "   5 to 8
I. Robinson, accommodates 12 ....   "   5 to 8

SPEONK, SUFFOLK CO., N. Y.—73 miles from N. Y.; situated on Great South Bay, and one mile from the ocean, which is reached every few minutes by boats run for the convenience of guests.

Rossmore House, accommodates 75 .... terms $6 to		$9
H. Rogers, accommodates 15 .... " 6 to		9
H. H. Rogers, accommodates 20 .... " 6 to		9
D. W. Ruland, accommodates 10 .... " 6 to		9

J. W. Tuthill offers accommodation for about 40. Grounds large and well shaded, and in full view of bay and ocean. Private conveyance free.

Terms $6 to $8

WEST HAMPTON, SUFFOLK CO., N. Y.—76 miles from N. Y. Surf and still-water bathing near by. This has long been a favored spot for those seeking a residence close by the sea.

Howell House, accommodates 75 .... terms $10 to		$12
Oneck House, accommodates 60 .... " 10 to		12
Mrs. C. Howell, accommodates 30 .... " 8 to		10
L. G. Rogers, accommodates 20 .... " 6 to		8
S. B. Topping, accommodates 25 .... " 6 to		8
Mrs. J. Young, accommodates 12 .... " 6 to		8
Halsey Rogers, accommodates 25 .... " 6 to		8
D. K. Haley, accommodates 20 .... " 8 to		10
Wm. Raynor, accommodates 20 .... " 6 to		8
H. F. Stevens, accommodates 15 .... " 6 to		8
Miss M. K. Foster, accommodates 30 .... " 6 to		8
E. Griffin, accommodates 20 .... " 6 to		8
Sarah Bulver, accommodates 18 .... " 6 to		8
W. C. Raynor, accommodates 12 .... " 6 to		8
N. Raynor, accommodates 15 .... " 6 to		8
C. R. Bishop, accommodates 10 .... " 6 to		8

QUOQUE, SUFFOLK CO., N. Y.—78 miles from N. Y. An old and comparatively well-known place, not far from the ocean, on a peninsula between the two Great South Bays. The air along this shore cannot be surpassed for its health-giving qualities. Surf and still water at hand.

Wells House, accommodates 60 .... terms $7 to		$10
Howell House, accommodates 90 .... " 7 to		10
Quantuc House, accommodates 40 .... " 7 to		10
Cooper House, accommodates 50 .... " 7 to		10
Well's Hotel, accommodates 40 .... " 7 to		10
Post House, accommodates 40 .... " 7 to		10
Foster House, accommodates 60 .... " 7 to		10
Hallock House, accommodates 50 .... " 7 to		10
Gardner House, accommodates 35 .... " 7 to		10
S. E. Jessup, accommodates 12 .... " 7 to		10
M. E. Griffin, accommodates 30 .... " 7 to		10

ATLANTICVILLE, SUFFOLK CO., N. Y.—Located 80 miles from N. Y., on Shinnecock Bay, and within short sail of the ocean.

B. S. Squires, accommodates 35 .... terms $7 to		$10
A. W. Jackson, accommodates 30 .... " 7 to		10
Halsey House, accommodates 40 .... " 7 to		10

John Carter, accommodates 20................terms $7 to 10
E. J. Downs, accommodates 15................ " 7 to 10
John Brown, accommodates 15........ ...... " 7 to 10

GOOD GROUND, SUFFOLK CO., N. Y.—84 miles from N. Y.,
and 2 miles from Shinnecock Bay, where excellent boating
and bathing can be had.

W. N. Lane, accommodates 30................terms $6 to $8
J. H. Corwin, accommodates 25... .... " 6 to 8
Mrs. S. R. Jackson, accommodates 10........ " 6 to 8
Mrs. A. Phillips, accommodates 12.......... " 6 to 8
Luther Hallock, accommodates 6............ " 5 to 6
S. C. Bellows, accommodates 12............. " 6 to 8

PONQUOQUE, SUFFOLK CO., N. Y.—2 miles from Good
Ground station, and located directly on Shinnecock Bay, in
full view of the ocean. The water attractions as here offered cannot be surpassed. Good bathing in both bay and
ocean.

Bay View House, accommodates 75..........terms $8 to $12
Well's House, accommodates 12............. " 8 to 12
Foster House, accommodates 40............. " 8 to 12
Field's Hotel, accommodates 30............. " 8 to 12

SOUTHAMPTON, SUFFOLK CO., N. Y.—91 miles from N. Y.
This well-known and popular resort is delightfully located
by the ocean. and affords every variety of pleasure usually
found at the sea side. * Air pure and bracing, and positively
healthy.

Post House, accommodates 45................terms $7 to $10
Ocean House, accommodates 25............. " 7 to 10
Huntington House, accommodates 25........ " 7 to 10
A. Robinson, accommodates 10............. " 7 to 10
H. N. Stein accommodates 15.............. " 7 to 10
E. Randall, accommodates 20.............. " 7 to 10
Mrs. Stanbrough, accommodates 20.......... " 7 to 10
Capt. Halsey, accommodates 15............ " 7 to 10
Mrs. H. White, accommodates 60........... " 7 to 10
B. J. Green, accommodates 60............. " 7 to 10
Miss Sandford, accommodates 25........... " 7 to 10
G. Whittaker, accommodates 25............ " 7 to 10
Miss J. Woolley, accommodates 20.......... " 7 to 10
Henry Reeves, accommodates 30............ " 7 to 10
S. Halsey, accommodates 20............... " 7 to 10
H. A. Fordam, accommodates 45............ " 7 to 10
E. C. Reeves, accommodates 25............ " 7 to 10
E. Post, accommodates 35................. " 7 to 10

WATERMILL, SUFFOLK CO., N. Y.—93 miles from N. Y., on
the south side of the island, pleasantly and conveniently
located near the ocean. Good boating, bathing and fishing
can be had in both surf and still water.

Point House, accommodates 35................terms $6 to $8
Mrs. N. Goodall, accommodates 40.......... " 6 to 8
J. A. Burnett, accommodates 10............ " 6 to 8
A. M. Benedict, accommodates 35 .... " 6 to 8

T. A. Halsey, accommodates 20	terms	$6 to	$8
P. S. Warren, accommodates 12	"	6 to	8
J. F. Halsey, accommodates 6	"	6 to	8
H. S. Rose, accommodates 8	"	6 to	8
H. M. Rose, accommodates 20	"	6 to	8
H. R. Halsey, accommodates 18	"	6 to	8
J. L. Cook, accommodates 15	"	6 to	8

BRIDGEHAMPTON, SUFFOLK CO., N. Y.—96 miles from N. Y. This is one of the most popular resorts on the east end of the Island, and well deserves its fame. It is located near the Ocean Beach, and a fresh water lake near by.

Hull's Hotel, accommodates 35	terms	$6 to	$8
C. S. Rogers, accommodates 30	"	6 to	8
Josiah Foster, accommodates 20	"	7 to	10
J. Ludlow, accommodates 25	"	6 to	8
J. A. Rogers, accommodates 15	"	7 to	8
J. M. Halsey, accommodates 12	"	8 to	10
H. R. Halsey, accommodates 20	"	8 to	10
A. J. Jennings, accommodates 20	"	8 to	10
H. S. Rogers, accommodates 20	"	8 to	10
E. J. Ludlow, accommodates 15	"	7 to	8
W. A. Corwin, accommodates 15	"	8 to	10
G. L. Hand, accommodates 12	"	7 to	8
S. Mulford, accommodates 10	"	7 to	8

EAST HAMPTON, SUFFOLK CO., N. Y.—Reached by stage from Bridgehampton or Sag Harbor ; it is a beautiful and favorite sea-side resort ; it is located on the surf and the ocean is in full view ; the bathing at this point is unusually fine.

J. D. Hedges accommodates 30	terms	$10
J. F. Gould, accommodates 25	"	10
J. Parsons, accommodates 40	"	10
Mrs. George Hand, accommodates 20	"	10
James P. Mulford, accommodates 20	"	10
Mrs. Cartwright, accommodates 10	"	10
R. M. Barker, accommodates 20	"	10
George Bushwell, accommodates 15	"	8
Mrs. H. Stratton, accommodates 15	"	10
H. A. Parsons, accommodates 40	"	10
H. B. Tuthill, accommodates 10	"	10
J. H. Parsons, accommodates 30	"	8
W. S. Gardner, accommodates 25	"	7
J. S. Osborn, accommodates 20	"	10
S. Gardner, accommodates 25	"	7
W. L. Osborn, accommodates 30	"	10

SAG HARBOR, SUFFOLK CO., N. Y.—103 miles from New York, on the extreme end of the railroad ; it is a very old town, and was for many years the headquarters for a large whale fishing interest ; houses are conveniently located near the water.

Nassau House, accommodates 30	terms	$7 to	$12
American House, accommodates 30	"	7 to	12

East End House, accommodates 25.......... " 7 to 12
Mrs. Douglas, accommodates 15............ " 7 to 12
Mrs. O. R. Wade, accommodates 15......... " 7 to 12
Mrs. M. J. Graham, accommodates 10....... " 7 to 12
G. S. Tooker, accommodates 10............ " 7 to 12

AMAGANSET, SUFFOLK CO., N. Y.—Located on the east end
end of the island and directly on the ocean ; reached by stage
from Sag Harbor.

B. H. Terry, accommodates 25.............terms $9
B. Barnes, accommodates 30............... "
Thomas Spier, accommodates 30........... " 7
N. Hand, accommodates 25................ " 8
T. H. Conklin, accommodates 15.......... " 8

FAR ROCKAWAY—BRANCH.

WOODSBURGH, QUEENS CO., N. Y.—18 miles from New
York, on the south side of the island, convenient to surf and
still-water bathing.

Pavilion Hotel, accommodates 400..........terms $10 to $15
Neptune House, accommodates 50........... " 10 to 15

OCEAN POINT, QUEENS CO., N. Y.—19 miles from N. Y., on
the south side of the island, and convenient to still water
and surf bathing.

J. R. Hicks, accommodates 8 ....terms $6 to $8
J. Carmen, accommodates 10 .... " 6 to 8

FAR ROCKAWAY, QUEENS CO., N. Y.—22 miles from N. Y.
It has a narrow, still water bay along its front, crossed by
boats n two minutes to the surf beach. Far Rockaway has
for years been a most favored summer resort. It is located
only four miles from the new hotel at Rockaway Beach,
which is the largest in the world.

United States, accommodates 300 ....terms $10 to $12
Coleman House, accommodates 200......... " 10 to 12
National Hotel, accommodates 100......... " 10 to 12
Pavilion Hotel, accommodates 150 .... " 10 to 12
Beach Hotel, accommodates 100 .... " 10 to 12
Union Surf Hotel, accommodates 75........ " 10 to 12
Foss Hotel, accommodates 75............. " 10 to 12
New York Hotel, accommodates 75 .... " — to —
Atlantic Hotel, accommodates 100......... " 8 to 10
Transatlantic Hotel, accommodates 70...... " 8 to 10
Neptune House, accommodates 75 .... " 8 to 10
Alhambra Hotel, accommodates 50......... " 8 to 10
Metropolitan Hotel, accommodates 15 ...... " 8 to 10
Rhode Island Houses, accommodates 25 .... " 8 to 15
Mansion House, accommodates 100......... " 10 to 15
Madison House, accommodates 38 .... " 8 to 10

CENTRAL OR MAIN LINE.

Along this delightful stretch from the head of Peconic Bay, one never tires for lack of amusement. The bathing is unrivaled, as are also the drives on the main land. The fishing is excellent, and in the fall it is a perfect paradise for sportsmen. A beautiful bay, almost at your very door, with the finest and safest boats in the world for the accommodation of those who are fond of sailing.

RIVERHEAD, SUFFOLK CO., N. Y.—74 miles from N. Y., at the head of Great Peconic Bay. A town of some importance, being the county seat of Suffolk Co.

Griffin Hotel, accommodates 75............terms	$8 to $10
Suffolk Hotel, accommodates 50 .... "	8 to 10
Long Island House, accommodates 70...... "	8 to 10

FLANDERS, SUFFOLK CO., N. Y.—Delightfully located at the head of Peconic Bay, and only a few minutes drive from the station at Riverhead. Grounds well shaded. Fruit and vegetables in abundance. Good boating and bathing.

Mrs. A. Benjamin, accommodates 20.............terms $6
Mrs. J. Squires, accommodates 20.................terms $6

JAMESPORT, SUFFOLK CO., N. Y.—79 miles from N. Y.; pleasantly located on Great Peconic Bay. It is a well known and popular resort, and affords many attractions for summer visitors.

Miamoque House, accommodates 35...........terms	$7 to $8
Bayside House, accommodates 30............... "	7 to 9
W. H. Corwin, accommodates 10............... "	6 to 8
W. Hallock, accommodates 12.................. "	6 to 8
Richard Albertson, accommodates 20........... "	6 to 8
I. F. Robinson, accommodates 8............... "	6 to 8
J. Woodhull, accommodates 15.................. "	6 to 8
S. R. Downs, accommodates 10 .... "	6 to 8
M. T. Benjamin, accommodates 27............. "	6 to 8

MATTITUCK, SUFFOLK CO., N. Y.—82 miles from N. Y.; and conveniently situated on Peconic Bay. Boating, bathing, and fishing is excellent.

Mattituck House, accommodates 50...........terms	$7 to $10
S. H. Tuthill, accommodates 10............... "	6 to 8
Mrs. R. H. Hazard, accommodates 10........ "	6 to 8
George A. Cox, accommodates 10............. "	6 to 8

CUTCHOGUE, SUFFOLK CO., N. Y.—85 miles from N. Y.; the houses are located two miles from depot at New Suffolk, which is situated directly on Great Peconic Bay, and affords the most delightful boating, bathing, and fishing.

New Suffolk Hotel, accommodates 90.........terms	$5 to $8
E. E. Horton, accommodates 15.............. "	5 to 8
I. I. Tuthill, accommodates 10 .... "	5 to 8

J. G. Tuthill, accommodates 25 .... terms $5 to 8
H. B. Halsey, accommodates 15 .... " 5 to 8
O. H. Tuthill, accommodates 15 .... " 5 to 8
F. R. Fanning, accommodates 20 .... " 5 to 8
J. B. Tuthill, accommodates 15 .... " 5 to 8
J. Jennings, accomodates 15 .... " 5 to 8

PECONIC, SUFFOLK CO., N. Y.—88 miles from N. Y., and pleasantly situated on Great Peconic Bay. Ground, high; fine views, and delightful boating, bathing, and fishing.

Mrs. H. M. Green, accommodates 10 .... terms, $5 to $7
J. M. Worth, accommodates 15 .... " 5 to 7
H. D. Horton. accommodates 5 .... " 5 to 7
N. L. Horton, accommodates 10 .... " 5 to 7

SOUTHOLD, SUFFOLK CO., N. Y.—90 miles from N. Y., and pleasantly located on Great Peconic Bay. The finest kind of fishing can be had at this point, and the boating and bathing is excellent. The country also affords good and attractive drives.

Judd's Hotel, accommodates 75 .... terms $7 to $10
Mrs. F. Maxwell, accommodates 40 .... " 7 to 10
J. C. Booth, accommodates 15 .... " 7 to 10
W. H. Tuthill, accommodates 15 .... " 7 to 10
S. B. Coney, accommodates 20 .... " 7 to 10
B. Wells, accommodates 10 .... " 7 to 10

GREENPORT, SUFFOLK CO., N. Y.—95 miles from N. Y.; built on the banks of the water, and located directly opposite Shelter Island. The boating and bathing at this point cannot be surpassed.

Clark House, accommodates 40 .... terms $10 to $12
Wyandauk House, accommodates 75 .... " 7 to 12
Peconic House, accommodates 80 .... " 7 to 12
Burr House, accommodates 20 .... " 7 to 12
Greenport House, accommodates 30 .... " 7 to 12
Booth House, accommodates 70 .... " 8 to 10
Mrs. Roe, accommodates 50 .... " 7 to 10
Mrs. M. J. Ashby, accommodates 10 .... " 7 to 10
Mrs. Ackerly, accommodates 10 .... " 7 to 10

SHELTER ISLAND, SUFFOLK CO., N. Y. Located directly opposite Greenport. This delightful place offers every variety of pleasure sought after by summer boarders. Good boating, bathing and fishing in the salt water, and those who wish can find plenty of amusement in the fresh water lakes which here abound.

Manhanset House, accommodates 200 .... terms $12 to $15
Prospect House, accommodates 150 .... " 12 to 15
Bay View House, accommodates 40 .... " 9 to 10
Laura B. Dickerson, accommodates 20 ...... " 6 to 8
Mrs. Nevins, accommodates 25 .... " 9 to 10
Mrs. Boardman, accommodates 20 .... " 9 to 10
Mrs. Waters, accommodates 30 .... " 9 to 10

ORIENT, SUFFOLK CO., N. Y.—Situated on the extreme east end of the north side of Long Island. Scenery and marine views unsurpassed. Close to water on all sides. Good boating, bathing and fishing. High hills and level plains in the rear. Orient is fast developing as a popular resort.

Rackett House, accommodates 30	terms	$8 to	$10
Brown House, accommodates 20	"	8 to	10
Vail House, accommodates 40	"		10
Mount Pleasant House, accommodates 40	"	8 to	10
Dyer House, accommodates 15	"	7 to	10
Orient Point House, accommodates 350	"	7 to	12
Bay House, accommodates 40	"	7 to	10

PORT JEFFERSON BRANCH.

OYSTER BAY, QUEENS CO., N. Y.—Pleasantly located on the north shore of Long Island, 4 miles from Syosset Station, which is 29 miles from N. Y. Good water conveniences are here offered.

Nassau House, accommodates 20	terms	$8 to	$10
Burrill Betts, accommodates 12	"	4 to	7
Mrs. Williams, accommodates 40	"	4 to	7
Mrs. Smith, accommodates 50	"	4 to	7
J. Wright, accommodates 30	"	4 to	7
Henry Sammis, accommodates 10	"	4 to	7
Mrs. A. Cheshire, accommodates 20	"	4 to	7
Miss Bayles, accommodates 10	"	4 to	7
Miss Waters, accommodates 30	"	4 to	7
R. Valentine, accommodates 10	"	4 to	7

COLD SPRING HARBOR, SUFFOLK CO., N. Y.—Located two miles from Woodbury Station, and directly on the Sound.

Laurelton Hall, accommodates 150	terms	$10 to	$12
Forest Lawn House, accommodates 50	"	8 to	10
Mrs. W. Wood, accommodates 20	"	6 to	7
David Rogers, accommodates 10	"	6 to	7
Gilbert Jayne, accommodates 8	"	6 to	7
George Dennison, accommodates 10	"	6 to	7
Sidney Titus, accommodates 12	"	6 to	7
J. B. Simonson, accommodates 15	"	6 to	7
W. Warren, accommodates 10	"	6 to	7

HUNTINGTON, SUFFOLK CO., N. Y.—37 miles from N. Y., on the north shore of Long Island, overlooking the Sound. Beautiful drives and attractive scenery.

Suffolk Hotel, accommodates 50	terms	$7 to	$10
Huntington House, accommodates 30	"	7 to	10
Mrs. H. J. Long, accommodates 10	"	7 to	8
C. J. Bancroft, accommodates 10	"	6 to	10
Mrs. M. J. Talmage, accommodates 12	"	6 to	10
Mrs. Hamilton, accommodates 10	"	6 to	10
Mrs. J. Johnson, accommodates 12	"	6 to	10

CENTREPORT, SUFFOLK CO, N. Y.—38 miles from N. Y.,
on the north shore of the Island, and convenient to the
Sound, where good boating and bathing may be had.

Centreport Hotel, accommodates 20	terms	$7 to	$8
Wm. H. Benham, accommodates 15	"	7 to	8
Joseph Irwin, accommodates 12	"	7 to	8
George Francis, accommodates 12	"	7 to	8
L. J. Martin, accommodates 40	"	7 to	8
Dr. James, accommodates 25	"	7 to	8

NORTHPORT, SUFFOLK CO., N. Y.—40 miles from N. Y.
Located directly on the Sound. Good drives and fine boating, bathing and fishing.

Northport House accommodates 40	terms	$7 to	$10
National Hall, accommodates 15	"	7 to	10
Mrs. Reilly, accommodates 20	"	6 to	8
Reuben Baldwin, accommodates 10	"	6 to	8
John Lewis, accommodates 12	"	6 to	8
P. H. Ackerly, accommodates 50	"	6 to	8
Mrs. J. Arthur, accommodates 10	"	6 to	8

SMITHTOWN, SUFFOLK CO., N. Y.—47 miles from N. Y., on
the north side of the island. A pleasant and attractive
spot for summer boarders.

Riverside Hotel, accommodates 30	terms	$6 to	$7
Mrs. E. Brush, accommodates 12	"	6 to	7
S. J. Halsey, accommodates 12	"	6 to	7

ST. JAMES, SUFFOLK CO., N. Y.—50 miles from N. Y.,
on the north side of the island, and located near the
Sound.

J. H. Jewell, accommodates 10	terms	$4 to	$7
Mrs. H. Smith, accommodates 6	"	4 to	7
H. Howell, accommodates 10	"	4 to	7
E. O. Smith, accommodates 7	"	4 to	7

STONY BROOK, SUFFOLK CO., N. Y.—54 miles from N. Y.;
located on the north side of the island. A pleasant and
attractive country, well suited to summer boarders.

Stony Brook Hotel, accommodates 75	terms	$7 to	$10
W. Jewell, accommodates 6	"	6 to	8
N. S. Hawkins, accommodates 6	"	6 to	8
D. W. Sherry, accommodates 10	"	6 to	8
Thomas S. Wells, accommodates 10	"	6 to	8
G. H. King, accommodates 10	"	6 to	8
J. Darling, accommodates 20	"	6 to	8
Mrs. Dickerson, accommodates 25	"	6 to	8
Chas. O'Dowd, accommodates 20	"	6 to	8
Mrs. Groesbeck, accommodates 15	"	6 to	8

SETAUKET, SUFFOLK CO., N. Y.—55 miles from N. Y.;
situated on the north shore of the island, directly on the
Sound. Good boating, bathing and fishing.

Mrs. H. Rowland, accommodates 20	terms	$6 to	$7
Mrs. O. W. Rogers, accommodates 12	"	6 to	7

Geo. Terrell, accommodates 12	terms	$6 to $7
Mrs. J. Howell, accommodates 12	"	6 to 7
J. Elderkins, accommodates 20	"	6 to 7
Miss Dominick, accommodates 12	"	6 to 7

PORT JEFFERSON, SUFFOLK CO., N. Y.—58 miles from N. Y., on the north shore of the island, and built directly on the Sound. A popular and attractive spot for summer boarders.

Townsend House, accommodates 35	terms	$7 to $10
Pt. Jefferson House, accommodates 35	"	7 to 10
Smith's Hotel, accommodates 20	"	6 to 8
D. Gildersleeve, accommodates 12	"	6 to 8
Mrs. E. P. Tooker, accommodates 12	"	6 to 8
Mrs. H. Tooker, accommodates 10	"	6 to 8
Mrs. C. L. Bayles, accommodates 20	"	6 to 8

NORTH SIDE DIVISION.

NEWTON, QUEENS CO., N. Y.—5 miles from N. Y., and nicely situated for summer boarders.

Newton House, accommodates 60	terms	$8 to $10
Mrs. S. Palmer, accommodates 10	"	8 to 10
Dick's Hotel, accommodates 20	"	6 to 7
B. G. Curtis, accommodates 15	"	6 to 7
Shueller's House, accommodates 15	"	6 to 7

FLUSHING, QUEENS CO., N. Y.—7 miles from N. Y.; conveniently located on the Sound, where good boating, bathing and fishing can be had.

Simmon's Hotel, accommodates 40	terms	$8 to $10
Fountain House, accommodates 20	"	8 to 10
P. C. Lewis, accommodates 10	"	6 to 7
Samuel B. Parsons, accommodates 15	"	10 to 15
Mrs. C. Lent, accommodates 25	"	8 to 10
Mrs. B. H. Benton, accommodates 10	"	8 to 10
Mrs. J. Jones, accommodates 12	"	8 to 10
Mrs. Treadwell, accommodates 10	"	6 to 10
Mrs. S. A. Hover, accommodates 10	"	8 to 10
Mrs. F. Henning, accommodates 8	"	6 to 8
Mrs. W. P. Foster, accommodates 10	"	8 to 10

COLLEGE POINT, QUEENS CO., N. Y.—10 miles from New York ; situated on the Sound, with every convenience and attraction for summer boarders.

Boulevard Hotel, accommodates 100	terms	$10 to $12
Pavilion, accommodates 20	"	8 to 10
Miller's Hotel, accommodates 15	"	8 to 10
J. Sanderson, accommodates 10	"	6 to 8
Darius Banks, accommodates 10	"	6 to 8
C. Heubell, accommodates 20	"	6 to 8
Gerlach's Hotel, accommodates 10	"	8 to 10
College Point Hotel, accommodates 20	"	8 to 10

WHITESTONE, QUEENS CO., N. Y.—11 miles from New York, and pleasantly located on the Sound. This is a popular resort for summer boarders.

Whitestone House, accommodates 150	terms	$10 to $12
Mrs. A. B. Wright, accommodates 10	"	6 to 8
Dr. G. F. Pitts, accommodates 15	"	6 to 8
Mrs. Hustis, accommodates 25	"	6 to 8
Mrs. S. B. Smith, accommodates 8	"	6 to 8
Mrs. Van Sicklin, accommodates 20	"	6 to 8

BAYSIDE, QUEENS CO., N. Y.—11½ miles from New York; convenient to the Sound, where good boating and bathing may be had.

Bayside Hotel, accommodates 80	terms	$10 to $12
B. J. Mannott, accommodates 20	"	6 to 8

GREAT NECK, QUEENS CO., N. Y.—14 miles from New York; pleasantly located near the Sound; good boating, bathing and fishing. The drives are excellent and country attractive.

Great Neck House, accommodates 100	terms	$10
Mrs. T. J. Walters, accommodates 10	"	$6 to 8
Mrs. Ward, accommodates 35	"	6 to 8
Sarah Holtz, accommodates 15	"	6 to 8
P. A. Edgett, accommodates 15	"	6 to 8
Private Br'k House, accommodates 12	"	6 to 8
P. O. Box 50, accommodates 10	"	6 to 8

GLEN COVE AND LOCUST VALLEY BRANCH.

ROSLYN, QUEEN'S CO., N. Y.—23 miles from N. Y.; conveniently situated near the Sound, where good boating, bathing and fishing can be had.

Roslyn Hotel, accommodates 25	terms	$7 to $10
Mansion House, accommodates 80	"	8 to 10
John Valentine, accommodates 25	"	5 to 7
Thomas Boyle, accommodates 20	"	5 to 6

GLEN COVE, QUEEN'S CO., N. Y.—28 miles from N. Y.; located on the Sound, where good boating, bathing and fishing are among the few attractions.

Glen Cove Hotel, accommodates 25	terms	$6 to $8
Mrs. M. A. Miller, accommodates 20	"	6 to 8
Mrs. W. Merritt, accommodates 15	"	6 to 8
Mrs. S. Y. Cole, accommodates 40	"	6 to 8
Thomas T. Jackson, accommodates 25	"	6 to 8
S. M. Titus, accommodates 12	"	6 to
George Searing, accommodates 20	"	6 to
E. S. Hendrickson, accommodates 20	"	6 to
Samuel Frost, accommodates 10	"	6 to 8
Willett Weeks, accommodates 10	"	6 to 8
Schleister Hotel, accommodates 15	"	6 to 8

LOCUST VALLEY, QUEENS CO., N. Y.—29 miles from N.Y., on the north shore of the Island, and conveniently located for boating, bathing and fishing. The drives are also good.

T. F. Underhill, accommodates 20............terms	$6 to	8
C. E. Feeks, accommodates 20................ "	6 to	8
F. Smith, accommodates 60................... "	6 to	8
B. F. Cock, accommodates 10................ "	6 to	8
Jno. Bayles, accommodates 10................ "	6 to	8
Misses Cock, accommodates 30..... .... "	6 to	8
Fa'm Mans'n House, accommodates 30........ "	6 to	8
Christian Ferling, accommodates 15.......... "	6 to	8

ENJOY A GOOD CUP OF

✛— T E A. —✛

3¼ lbs. of our celebrated

SUN-SUN CHOP TEA,

The Finest and Most Beneficial imported, sent by mail on receipt of $2.50, postage paid. It is a Black Tea, with a Green Tea flavor. Recommended to Suit all Tastes. Sample of any of our Teas by mail on receipt of 6 cents.

Postage Stamps taken.

Good Teas, 30c., 35c. and 40c. Excellent Teas, 50 and 60c. All Express paid on $5.00 Tea orders.

On $20 TEA Orders we will deduct 15 per cent. off and Pay ALL EXPRESS CHARGES.

HOTELS, BOARDING HOUSE KEEPERS AND LARGE CONSUMERS will do well by giving our Teas and Coffees a trial. No house can compete with us. Send for Price List and get our latest terms.

THE GREAT AMERICAN TEA CO., Importers,

P. O. Box 289.   Nos. 31 & 33 Vesey Street, New York.

THE CATSKILL MOUNTAINS

AND POINTS REACHED VIA

Ulster and Delaware Railroad

FROM RONDOUT.

The world-wide reputation of the Catskill Mountains are too well known to require detail mention here. The lovers of nature may find among their numerous peaks scenery of the grandest character. Those in search of fishing or hunting will find enough to keep them busy. Day or night boats from New York connect with trains at Rondout, a landing on the Hudson, for all points amid this region.

WEST HURLEY, ULSTER CO., N. Y.—9 miles from Rondout; elevation 530 feet above tide water; fine mountain scenery; good fishing and hunting; take stage from this point for Woodstock.

A. A. Castel, accommodates 4 .... terms	Apply.
M. J. Hardenburgh, accommodates 28 .... "	$6 to $8
D. C. Griffin, accommodates 18 .... "	7
Geo. E. Row, accommodates 4 .... "	5

WOODSTOCK, ULSTER CO., N. Y.—5 miles from West Hurley station. At this point is reached Overlook Mountain, one of the highest peaks of the range. Elevation 3,000 feet.

T. G. Montgomery, accommodates 8 .... terms	$5 to $7
Benjamin Hoffman, accommodates 15 .... "	apply.
J. Beekman, accommodates 15 .... "	5 to 7
A. Elvyn, accommodates 15 .... "	5 to 7
A. Longyear, accommodates 10 .... terms	$5 to $7
S. Thompson, accommodates 15 .... "	5 to 7
E. Snyder, accommodates 8 .... "	5 to 7
O. N. Risley, accommodates 15 .... "	5 to 7
O. Snyder, accommodates 6 .... "	6 to 7
Overlook Mountain House, accommodates 250. "	apply.
Geo. Mead, accommodates 35 .... "	"

OLIVE, ULSTER CO., N. Y.—12 miles from Rondout; elevation 500 feet. This is a very popular and attractive resort. Good fishing and hunting can be had.

George Mayland, accommodates 15 .... terms	$3 to $6
A. Simmons, accommodates 15 .... "	3 to 6
Andrew Markle, accommodates 10 .... "	3 to 6

P. H. Lasher, accommodates 50...............terms	$6 to	$9
J. Elmendorf, accommodates 10.............. "	3 to	6
Dr. A. C. Hall, accommodates 15.............. "		6
Geo. Brower, accommodates 15 .... "	3 to	6
J. Davis, accommodates 15.................. "	3 to	6
Wallace Lee, accommodates 15 .... "	3 to	4
Isaac Winchell, accommodates 15 .... "	3 to	5

BROADHEADS BRIDGE, ULSTER CO., N. Y.—17 miles from Rondout and close by the well-known "Bishop's Falls." Elevation above tide water 500 feet.

Calvin Case, accommodates 20 ....terms	$6 to	$8
Isaac Bloom, accommodates 25................ "	7 to	8
D. P. Short, accommodates 25 .... "	apply.	
D. J. Adams, accommodates 25 .... "	7 to	8
I. S. Bloom, accommodates 25 .... "	7 to	8
J. L. Broadhead, accommodates 12........... "	apply.	
Stephen H. Broadhead, accommodates 25.... "	"	
J. N. Berryan, accommodates 10............. "	"	
Jacob S. Lockwood, accommodates 12 ...,.... "	"	
Oliver Davis, accommodates 10 .... "	"	

OLIVE BRIDGE, ULSTER CO., N. Y.—2 miles from Broadhead's Bridge station. High and healthy: good fishing and hunting.

Lewis Hollister, accommodates 12...........terms	$6 to	$8
Charles H. Davis, accommodates 8........... "	apply.	
Hugh Lock, accommodates 8................. "	"	
Henry W. Winans, accommodates 6.......... "	"	

BROWN'S STATION, ULSTER CO., N. Y.—15 miles from Rondout, with an elevation above tide-water of 525 feet. Good fishing and hunting.

Philip H. Lasher, accommodates 50...........terms	$7 to	$8
Albert Brown, accommodates 40............. "	apply.	
Egbert Dedrick, accommodates 30.......... . "	"	
William Elmendorf, accommodates 10 .... "	"	
Addison Stratton, accommodates 30 .... "	"	

SHOKAN, ULSTER CO., N. Y.—18 miles from Rondout; elevation above tide-water, 533 feet. Leave the cars at this station for West Shokan.

Jacob Krom, accommodates 15...............terms	$6 to	$8
John Windrum, accommodates 15 .... "		6
D. C. Davis, accommodates 10............... "		6
J. M. Eckert, accommodates 10............... "	apply.	
N. Boice, accommodates 10................. "	"	
S. Markle, accommodates 10................. "	6 to	8
J. M. Burgher, accommodates 20............. "	7 to	14

WEST SHOKAN, ULSTER CO., N. Y.—One and a half miles from Shokan station. A pleasant and delightful summer retreat, amid mountain scenery.

Nelson Kron, accommodates 25...............terms	$6 to	$8
E. R. Matthews, accommodates 10............. "	apply.	

C. C. Winne, accommodates 25............terms $6 to $8
D. N. Davis, accommodates 10............. "   6 to 8
Mrs. C. M. Winne, accommodates 15......... "   3 to 6
J. M. Burgher, accommodates 25............ "   6 to 8
T. Eckert, accommodates 25................ "   6 to 8

BOICEVILLE, ULSTER CO., N. Y.—21 miles from Rondout. Elevation 650 feet.

H. W. Davis, accommodates 20.............terms $6 to $7
P. A. Woolven, accommodates 15... .... "   6 to 7
John Hull, accommodates 15... .... "   apply.
A. Howland, accommodates 10.............. "   "

MOUNT PLEASANT, ULSTER CO., N. Y.—24 miles from Rondout. Elevation above tide water 700 feet. Take stage from this point for The Corner, and Lake Hill.

Mrs. S. Lamson, accommodates 20.. . ...terms $6 to $8
La Dew Farm, accommodates 40............. "   6 to 8

THE CORNER, ULSTER CO., N. Y.—One mile and a half from Mt. Pleasant station. A pleasantly located and popular resort. Good fishing and hunting.

Lamson House, accommodates 40...........terms $8 to $10
S. S. Randall, accommodates 8........... " $6 to $7
Cockburn House, accommodates 75......... "   "
W. Schumacker, accommodates 40.......... "   "
Doris Winnie, accommodates 15........... "   8
H. B. Hudler, accommodates 20........... "   "

LAKE HILL, ULSTER CO., N. Y.—Four miles from Mt. Pleasant station. High and pleasant location. A good fishing and hunting region.

R. R. Wilbur, accommodates 20...........terms $6
Charles Short. accommodates 20.......... "   7
Abraham Quick, accommodates 12.......... "   6
S. A. Mosher, accommodates 10........... "   7
B. E. Hasbrouck, accommodates 16........ " $6 to 8
L. Pine, accommodates 15................ "   Apply.
J. G. Waters, accommodates 15........... "   "
E. D. Staples, accommodates 12.......... "   "
Mrs. J. Wilmot, accommodates 12......... "   "

PHŒNICIA, ULSTER CO., N. Y.—27 miles from Rondout. Elevation 798 feet above tide water. This is a well-known and popular resort and also a point of departure for points further up in the Mountains.

A. Connelly, accommodates 10............terms $8 to $10
O. Hamilton, accommodates 15 .... "   apply.
Tremper House, accommodates 250......... "   "
Valley House, accommodates 65 .... "   7 to 10
D. W. Preston, accommodates 20.......... "   6 to 8
J. D. Phillips, accommodates 25......... "   apply.
O. B. Crosby, accommodates 12........... "   "
Amos Connelly, accommodates 15.......... "   7 to 8
Edward Lane, accommodates 25............ "   apply.

HUNTER, GREEN CO., N. Y.—14 miles from Phœnicia on the Stoney Clove R. R. Located amid wild mountain scenery, good gunning and fishing. Take stage from this station also for Tannersville, Hensonville, Union and Windham.

Mrs. Goodrich, accommodates 16	terms	$8 to	$10
L. Whittaker, accommodates 12	"	6 to	8
William Blair, accommodates 14	"	7 to	10
Wm. H. Mansfield, accommodates 12	"	7 to	8
H. C. Van Pelt, accommodates 100	"	7 to	10
H. E. Bedell, accommodates 15	"	7 to	12
Mrs. A. Attwater, accommodates 10	"	7 to	12
W. F. Green, accommodates 10	"	7 to	10
W. J. Rusk & Son, accommodates 65	"	8 to	10
W. O. Douglas, accommodates 15	"	7 to	10
Breeze Lawn, accommodates 100	"	7 to	10
L. Lindsey, accommodates 25	"	7 to	10

TANNERSVILLE, GREEN CO., N. Y.—3 miles from Hunter station on the Stony Clove R. R. Elevation 2,000 feet above tide water, is a wild attractive county; good hunting and fishing.

Michail Gillespie, accommodates 25	terms	Apply.
Dennis Brown, accommodates 20	,,	"
Lester, accommodates 10	"	"
William Smith, accommodates 10	"	$7 to $10
Mrs. James Brown, accommodates 50	"	apply.
Mrs. L. Craig, accommodates 15	"	"
Rufus Shower's Villa, accommodates 15	"	"
G. N. Eggliston, accommodates 70	"	"
Daniel McGrath, accommodates 8	"	"
Shultz Hotel, accommodates 50	"	"
Home Boarding House, accommodates 30	"	"
Mrs. Alex. Hemsley, accommodates 60	"	"
W. Wooden, accommodates 30	"	"
Dykman, accommodates 10	"	"
A. T. Haines, accommodates 40	"	"
Frank Eggleston, accommodates 12	"	"
Colonel Roggen, accommodates 150	"	7 to 10
Isaac Showers, accommodates 8	"	apply.
Mrs. Parker, accommodates 8	"	"
James Flannigan, accommodates 25	"	"
Ezra Howard, accommodates 15	"	"
Dr. Haner, accommodates 8	"	"
Dr. Payne, accommodates 15	"	"
S. S. Mulford, accommodates 150	"	"
B. McAlinda, accommodates 10	"	"
Edgar Layman, accommodates 25	"	"
M. O'Hara, accommodates 15	"	"
Augustus Layman, accommodates 25	"	"
James Haine, accommodates 10	"	"
Rose Cottage, accommodates 20	"	"
Cornelius H. Legg, accommodates 30	"	"
Owen Glennon, accommodates 50	"	"

John O'Hara, accommodates 40 ....terms   Apply.
Miles Hines, accommodates 75 ....   "   "
Vista, accommodates 40 ....   "   "
C. W. Haines, accommodates 90 ....   "   "
Jessie Haines accommodates 25 ....   "   "
Hallinbeck, accommodates 75 ....   "   "
Jerry Haines, accommodates 10 ....   "   "
J. E. Haines, accommodates 10 ....   "   "
Fred. Ingals, accommodates 20 ....   "   "
George Read, accommodates 30 ....   "   "
Nelson Schribner, accommodates 60 ....   "   "
Ed. Adams, accommodates 8 ....   "   "
John Schribner, accommodates 15 ....   "   "
Jerry Yager, accommodates 20 ....   "   "
Harding's New Mountain House, accommo-
    dates 500 ....   "   "
C. L. Beach, accommodates 400 ....   "   "

WINDHAM, GREEN CO., N. Y.—8 miles from Hunter Station on the Stony Clove R. R., and 25 miles from Catskill. Unsurpassed mountain scenery; good hunting and fishing.

W. H. Moon, accommodates 15 ....terms   Apply.
D. C. Tibbals, accommodates 15 ....   "   "
R. Macomber, accommodates 15 ....   "   "
L. S. Graham, accommodates 15 ....   "   "
H. Bagley, accommodates 15 ....   "   "
A. R. Mott, accommodates 15 ....   "   "
Brockett & Scurir, accommodates 30 ....   "   "
George Graham, accommodates 25 ....   "   "
L. I. Smalling, accommodates 20 ....   "   "
Dr. P. I. Stanley, accommodates 20 ....   "   "
R. Steele, accommodates 20 ....   "   "
Dr. Mead, accommodates 20 ....   "   "
O. R. Coe, accommodates 50 ....   "   "
I. B. Steele, accommodates 15 ....   "   "
J. Mead, accommodates 25 ....   "   "
G. M. Thorpe, accommodates 15 ....   "   "
E. Graham, accommodates 15 ....   "   "
M. Riggs, accommodates 20 ....   "   "
Ira Day, accommodates 20 ....   "   ',
N. Steele, accommodates 25 ....   "   "
Wm. De Lamater, accommodates 15 ....   "   "
M. McLean, accommodates 25 ....   "   "
D. B. Steele, accommodates 15 ....   "   "
S. Wunger, accommodates 75 ....   "   "
George Melich, accommodates 30 ....   "   "
E. Bump, accommodates 35 ....   "   "
Addison Steele, accommodates 30 ....   "   "
B. Bronson, accommodates 15 ....   "   "
O. Bronson, accommodates 15 ....   "   "
D. Richmond, accommodates 15 ....   "   "
S. L. Munson, accommodates 40 ....   "   "

J. Soper, accommodates 50................terms   Apply.
Mrs. Loughran, accommodates 30..........   "   "
Elbert Osborn, accommodates 35..........   "   "
L. Turk, accommodates 25...............   "   "
Samuel Pelham, accommodates 25..........   "   "
I. Butts, accommodates 35................   "   "

EAST WINDHAM, GREEN CO. N. Y.—10 miles from Hunter Station, on the Stony Clove R. R., located high up in the mountains, 3,000 feet above tide water.

Grand View Mt. House, accommodates 100..terms   Apply.
A. Lamoreau, accommodates 40............   "   Moderate.
M. E. Sherman, accommodates 30..........   " $6 to 8

FOX HOLLOW, ULSTER CO., N. Y.—32 miles from Rondout, with an elevation above tide water of 1,000 feet.

O. J. Hamilton, accommodates 10..........terms $6 to 10
J. Whitney, accommodates 25.............   "   7 to 10
G. Whitney, accommodates 12.............   "   6 to 12
J. Lawler, accommodates 30..............   "   7 to 10
G. Ennis, accommodates 30..............   "   7 to 10
S. D. Souls, accommodates 15............   "   6 to 10
N. Brown, accommodates 35..............   "   6 to 9

SHANDAKEN, ULSTER CO., N. Y.—33 miles from Rondout. Elevation, 1,060 feet; good fishing and hunting. This is one of the most popular points along the road.

John Lawler, accommodates 30........ ....terms $7 to 8
Henry Griffith, accommodates 15..........   "   apply.
Thomas Hill, Jr., accommodates 30.........   "   "
F. B. Lament, accommodates 60............   " $7 to 10
C. Ostrander, accommodates 40..........   "   4 to 8
N. Brown, accommodates 25..............   "   apply.
J. Whitney, accommodates 20.... ....   "   "

WESTKILL, GREEN CO., N. Y.—7 miles from Shandaken Station, and 1,200 feet above tide-water. Good fishing and hunting.

W. Van Valkenburgh, accommodates 20.....terms $7 to $ 8
S. L. Ford, accommodates 30..............   "   apply
S. Deyoe, accommodates 40..............   "   6 to 8
D. H. Hubbard, accommodates 28..........   "   7 to 8
Deyoe House, accommodates 40............   "   8 to 10
Echo Notch House, accommodates 36.......   "   8 to 10
Shady Lawn House, accommodates 48.......   "   8 to 10*

LEXINGTON, GREEN CO., N. Y.—10 miles from Shandaken Station, with an elevation of 1,600 feet, and at the base of the Vly Mountains, one of the highest Peaks in the Catskill Mountains. It is convenient to boating, fishing, and hunting.

R. C. Deyo, accommodates 25..............terms $7 to $10
A. Deyo, accommodates 20................   "   7 to 10
S. C. Chamberlin, accommodates 30........   "   7 to 8

I. Kipp, accommodates 30 .... terms $7 to $8
Mrs. R. Douglass, accommodates 50 .... " 8 to 9
Mrs. R. Pettit, accommodates 10 .... " apply.
Dr. E. L. Ford, accommodates 50 .... " 8 to 10
B. O'Hara, accommodates 70 .... " apply.
J, S. Thompson, accommodates 20 .... " 7 to 8
S. Martin, accommodates 20 .... " 7 to 8

BIG INDIAN, ULSTER CO., N. Y.—36 miles from Rondout, and
has an elevation of 1,209 feet above the sea.

Mrs. C. Griffin, accommodates 4 .... terms $4
A. R. Mulnix, accommodates 15 .... " 6
J. S. Smith, accommodates 15 .... " Reasonable
E. Maybo, accommodates 15 .... " "
Slide Mt. House, accommodates 40 .... " "
Byron Dutcher, accommodates 40 .... " "
Francis Burnham, accommodates 10 .... " "
Geo. S. Misner, accommodates 35 .... " "

PINE HILL, ULSTER CO., N. Y.—39 miles from Rondout. Elevation 1,660 feet. Fishing and hunting.

C. C. Blodget, accommodation 45 ...... terms Apply.
Guijon House, accommodates 200 .... " $7 to $10
Glen Hall, accommodates 50 .... " 7 to 10
Mrs. Floyd, accommodates 50 .... " 7 to 10
J. Hasbrouck, accommodates 20 .... " 7
T. S. Lamment, accommodates 20 .... " apply.
D. T. Winter, accommodates 20 .... " "

SUMMIT, ULSTER CO., N. Y.—41 miles from Rondout. Elevation 1,886 feet.

Grand Hotel, accommodates 450 .... terms Apply.
W. H. Whispell, accommodate 35 .... " "

GRIFFINS CORNERS, DELAWARE CO., N. Y.—44 miles
from Rondout; elevation 1,516 feet; beautiful scenery, good
fishing and hunting.

Hatfield mansion, accommodates 40 .... terms Apply.
G. H. Jones, accommodates 24 .... " $6 to $7
J. M. Blish, accommodates 20 .... " 6 to 7
O. Vermilyea, accommodates 30 .... " apply.
T. C. Banker, accommodates 25 .... " "
C. S. Minor, accommodates 40 .... " "
T. Lomas Barrett, accommodates 25 .... " "
Allen Lasher, accommodates 20 .... " "

ARKVILLE, DELAWARE CO., N. Y.—Located 48 miles from
Rondout, and has an elevation of 1,344 feet.

L. W. Longyear, accommodates 30 .... terms $6
M. A. Lasher, accommodates 40 .... " moderate.
H. B. Kelley, accommodates 30 .... " "
S. Cole, accommodates 30 .... " "
Mrs. D. Hull, accommodates 15 .... " $6 to 8

ROXBURY, DELAWARE CO., N. Y.—59 miles from Rondout; elevated 1,497 feet; fine views; good fishing and hunting.

P. F. Hubbell, accommodates 25	terms Apply	
O. P. More, accommodates 20	"	"
L. Shutts, accommodates 10	"	"
G. M. Bouton, accommodates 20	" $6 to $8	
J. M. Dudley, accommodates 15	"	7
W. D Powell, accommodates 25	"	apply.
R. Hamma, accommodates 18	"	"
J. N. Rowland, accommodates 15	"	5 to 8

GRAND GORGE, DELAWARE CO., N. Y.—65 miles from Rondout, with an elevation of 1,570 feet. Parties for Prattsville and Gilboa will take stage from this point.

W. P. More, accommodates 10	terms $6 to $9

GILBOA, SCHOHARIE CO., N. Y.—3 miles from Grand Gorge Station, and "high up" in the mountains; fishing and hunting.

Frank Hagadorn, accommodates 30	terms Apply.	
W. H. Becker, accommodates 15	" $6 to $7	
Addison Hagadorn, accommodates 15	"	apply.
A. G. Baldwin, accommodates 12	"	"
H. A. Griffin, accommodates 12	"	"
Mrs. C. Buckingham, accommodates 10	"	5 to 7
M. D. Spencer, accommodates 10	"	5 to 7

PRATTSVILLE, GREEN CO., N. Y., 6 miles from Grand Gorge Station, with an elevation of 1,700 feet. Fine moun scenery, good hunting and fishing.

Devasego House, accommodates 75	terms	$6 to $7
J. L. Rapyelea, accommodates 50	"	6 to 7
C. R. Newcomb, accommodates 28	"	apply.
D. W. Ferguson, accommodates 15	"	7 to 8
J. Judson, Jr., accommodates 10	"	7 to 8
Paul Reader, accommodates 125	"	apply.
Peckham & Rappleyea, accommodates 75	"	"
M. H. Stryker, accommodates 70	"	7 to 9
Geo. Sax, accommodates 40	"	apply.

SOUTH GILBOA, SCHOHARIE CO., N. Y.—71 miles from Rondout, with an elevation of 1,845 feet. Good hunting, fishing and boating.

E. A. Sowles, accommodates 20	terms	$6 to $8
John Chichester, accommodates 10	"	6 to 7
H. & D. Brewster, accommodates 10	"	6 to 7
Mrs. E. Stevens, accommodates 10	"	apply.
Robert Conrow, accommodates 10	"	6 to 7
C. H. Mayham, accommodates 10	"	6 to 7

STAMFORD, DELAWARE CO. N. Y.—74 miles from Rondout, the terminus of the U. & D. R. R. It is located on the East Branch of the Delaware River, at an elevation of 1,767 feet above tide water.

A. F. Bartlett, accommodates 60	terms	Apply.
J. Hamilton, accommodates 20	"	"
E. J. Brockway, accommodates 20	"	"

A. L. Churchill, accommodates 25 .... terms	Apply.
J. R. Clark, accommodates 15 .... "	$6 to $8
S. E. Churchill, accommodates 40 .... "	6 to 8
E. S. Brownevill, accommodates 12 .... "	7
J. B. Griffin, accommodates 12 .... "	apply.
Mrs. G. Leonard, accommodates 8 .... "	"
J. W. Maynard, accommodates 25 .... "	"
F. Warne, accommodates 8 .... "	7
F. G. Rulifson, accommodates 12 .... "	7
L. E. Kendall, accommodates 18. .... "	apply.
W. F. Spencer, accommodates 12 .... "	"
J. H. McKee, accommodates 14 .... "	"
J. B. Gaylord, accommodates 12 .... "	"
Geo. B. Moore, accommodates 12 .... "	"
B. C. Smith, accommodates 12 .... "	"

HOBART, DELAWARE CO., N. Y.—4 miles from Stamford Station, and located on the East Branch of the Delaware River. Elevation 1,516 feet.

Dr. J. Reynolds, accommodates 15 .... terms	$7
G. A. Stephens, accommodates 15 .... "	apply.
D. R. Grant, accommodates 15 .... "	"
W. B. Grant, accommodates 15 .... "	"

Along the Erie Railway.

Comparatively few of the people in New York city, annually seeking summer rest or recreation, have any proper idea of the charming views at nearly every point along the entire line of this great quadruple track of iron, from the Atlantic Ocean to Lake Erie. There is a grandeur of scenery throughout all this broad region of craggy rocks and lofty hills, with shady glens and beautiful streams in valleys of green—surpassed only by the sublime efforts of nature manifested in the Rocky Mountains. Here the atmosphere is always pure—the water untainted, and insective pests unknown. Indeed the entire line of the Erie Railway is a grand field of charming study, and a greater part of the entire section is famous for its hunting and fishing. The lover of trout, bass fishing, and pickerel fishing, will find ample field for the gratification of his passion among the creeks, lakes, and rivers, while the latter season opens unrivaled haunts for the hunter, with his fowling piece or rifle, his setter or deer hound.

Main Line.

RUTHERFORD PARK, BERGEN CO., N. J.; 9½ miles from N. Y. A beautiful village, with many attractions and in close proximity to the Passaic River.

Rutherford House, accommodates 20........terms	$5 to $10
Riverside Hotel, accommodates 15.......... "	8 to 10
Mrs. Van Riper, accommodates 20......... "	6 to 10
Lyndhurst, accommodates 30............... "	10 to 12

PASSAIC BRIDGE, PASSAIC CO., N. J.--11 miles from N. Y.; a pleasant and attractive place for summer boarders.

Park Hotel, accommodates 150.............terms	$9 to $12
John S. Conkling, accommodates 12....... "	8 to 10
F. R. Towner, accommodates 15.......... "	Apply.
D. H. Spier, accommodates 20............. "	apply.
B. Hadley, accommodates 20............... "	apply.

PASSAIC, PASSAIC CO., N. J.—12 miles from N. Y. ; a delightful city, on an elevated point in the heart of the Passaic Valley. Fine boating and fishing in the Passaic River.

Mrs. J. T. Van Iderstine, accommodates 15.terms	Apply.
Mrs. Van Auken, accommodates 20........ "	apply.
P. W. Doremus, accommodates 15......... "	apply.
Mrs. Hardwicke, accommodates 20......... "	apply.

CLIFTON, PASSAIC CO., N. J.—13½ miles from N. Y.; a charming spot, within easy walking distance of Dundee Lake, a popular resort for boating and fishing.

Clifton Grove House, accommodates 40.....terms $7 to $10

LAKE VIEW, PASSAIC CO., N. J.—15 miles from N. Y. ; a quiet and attractive village, overlooking the Passaic Valley at Dundee Lake.

Auquackanonk House, accommodates	Apply.
Mrs. Britton, on the Hill,	apply.
Lake View Hotel, accommodates 20........terms	$8 to $10

HAWTHORN, PASSAIC CO., N. J.—19 miles from N. Y. ; on elevated ground, in good farming country. Fishing and boating in the river.

A. S. Beaks, accommodates 8..............terms	$6 to	$8
Mrs. James Fenner, accommodates 10...... "	6 to	8
C. J. Jackerman, accommodates 8......... "	6 to	8
P. D. Westervelt, accommodates 4......... "	6 to	8

RIDGEWOOD, BERGEN CO., N. J.—22 miles from N. Y,, in the heart of the Paramus Valley. Good views and the best of drives.

Andrew Hopper, accommodates 10 ....terms	$6 to	$8
G. J. Hopper, accommodates 10.............. "	6 to	8

HOHOKUS, BERGEN CO., N. J.—24 miles from N. Y. A picturesque and interesting spot in the Paramus Valley. Fine drives and walks.

A. Dickie, accommodates 15.................terms	$6 to	$8
J. A. Osborne, accommodates 12............... "	6 to	8
Mrs. Van Amburgh, accommodates 12........ "	6 to	8
J. J. Voorhees, accommodates 12.............. "	6 to	8
H. C. Dennett, accommodates 20 .... "	6 to	8
J. N. Lemon, accommodates 15 .... "	6 to	8
J, A. Zabriskie, accommodates 6............. "	6 to	8

ALLENDALE, BERGEN, N. J.—26 miles from N. Y. A delightful village; attractive surroundings; pure air and water.

P. Powell, accommodates 10 ....terms	$6 to	$8
J. J. Morrison, accommodates 15............... "	6 to	8
William Ackerman, accommodates 15......... "	6 to	8
A. De Baum, accommodates 20............ .... "	6 to	8
A. W. Ackerman, accommodates 15 .... "	6 to	8

RAMSEY'S, BERGEN CO., N. J.—28 miles from N.Y. On high
ground, at the outlet of the Ramapo Valley. Trout streams
in the mountains easy of access. Healthful; good drives,
and very attractive.

Fowler House, Sportsmen's Hotel. Guides furnished.

A. De Baun, accommodates 20	terms	$6 to $8
Shady Lawn House, accommodates 25	"	6 to 8
Mrs. D. Valentine, accommodates 10	"	apply.
Mrs. J. W. Valentine, accommodates 10	"	"
Rev. E. Deyo, accommodates 10	"	reasonable
L. Von Xiczinesky, accommodates 25	"	"
Isaac Ramsey, accommodates 10	"	"
A. A. Ackerman, accommodates 15	"	"

MAHWAH, BERGEN CO., N. J.—29 miles from N. Y. Situate
among rugged hills that rise in purple ranks on every side.

Mountain View House, accommodates 20	terms	$7 to $8
Mahwah House, accommodates 20	"	7 to 8
Mrs. D. W. Hopper, accommodates 15	"	8

SUFFEREN, ROCKLAND CO., N. Y.—32 miles from N. Y.
Many natural attractions surround this place. It is located
at the base of the Southern Highlands of the Hudson. Good
fishing and hunting.

L. D. Coe, accommodates 20	terms	$8 to $10
R. Blauvett, accommodates 8	"	7 to 8
Mrs. E. Nicholson, accommodates 8	"	8 to 10
A. Coe, accommodates 10	"	8 to 10
Mt. Terrace House, accommodates 50	"	8 to 12
Alvin Johnson, accommodates 8	"	8 to 10
C. A. Wanamaker, accommodates 6	"	8 to 10
Charles Sufferen, accommodates 35	"	10 to 12
Abbott Cooper, accommodates 30	"	8 to 10
H. A. Wanamaker, accommodates 20	"	8 to 10
A. E. Ivers, accommodates 30	"	7 to 9

SLOATSBURGH, ROCKLAND CO., N. Y.—36 miles from New
York, in a famous sporting region. Surrounded by lakes,
streams and hills. Lakes 1,000 feet above tide water ; good
drives.

J. T. Allen, accommodates 30	terms	$10
J. W. Ten Eyck, accommodates 50	"	8 to $10
J. J. Barbaro, accommodates 10	"	8 to 10
Sloat Mansion, accommodates 40	"	7 to 9

TURNER'S, ORANGE CO., N. Y.—48 miles from New York ;
fine mountain scenery, good drives, fishing and hunting.

Mrs. P. Turner, accommodates 20	terms	$8 to $14
C. Ford, accommodates 25	"	6 to 8
A. Chase, accommodates 12	"	8 to 9
Mrs. McKelrey, accommodates 15	"	7 to 10
Peter Turner, accommodates 20	"	8 to 10
N. Starkweather, accommodates 25	"	8 to 12

```
Gilbert Turner, accommodates 20 ........... terms   $6 to   $8
W. S. Smith, accommodates 30 .............    "      6 to    8
F. H. Martin, accommodates 15 .............    "      6 to   10
```

MONROE, ORANGE CO., N, Y.—50 miles from New York, among the dairy farms of Southern Orange. Lakes, mountains and streams near by.

```
Seven Spring Mountain House, accomdates 400 ................................. terms  $10 to  $15
Grantic House, accommodates 40 ...........    "      8 to   10
C. W. Mapes, accommodates 12 ............     "      7 to   10
Mrs. E. C. Jones, accommodates 12 ........    "      7 to   10
J. D. Ludlum, accommodates 25 ............    "      8 to   10
A. W. Roe, accommodates 12 ...............    "      7 to   10
A. Carpenter, accommodates 8 .............    "      7 to   10
Monroe House, accommodates 50 ...........     "      8 to   10
W. R. Conkling, accommodates 16 .........     "      6 to    7
P. C. Hager, accommodates 10 .............    "      6 to    8
Uriah Croson, accommodates 12 ...........     "      6 to   10
Wm. Sutherland, accommodates 12 .........     "      6
```

OXFORD, ORANGE CO., N. Y.—52 miles from New York. Fine scenery, lakes and streams, pure air and water have made this a popular retreat.

```
J. M. Seeley, accommodates 20 ........... terms    $5 to   $8
A. H. Lawrence, accommodates 15 ........     "      4 to    8
B. T. Tuthill, accommodates — .........      "      — to   —
Miss A. Y. Clark, accommodates 30 ........    "      5 to    8
Joseph W. Youngs, accommodates — ......      "      5 to   10
```

CRAIGVILLE, ORANGE CO., N. Y.—56 miles from New York. A delightful place among farms. Plenty of fishing both in streams and lakes.

```
J. W. Holmes, accommodates 20 ........... terms    $6 to   $8
J. Wickham, accommodates 8 ..............     "      6 to    8
Mrs. T. Cameron, accommodates 20 ........     "        apply.
```

GOSHEN, ORANGE CO., N. Y.—59 miles from New York. The stock farms in and around Goshen are celebrated all over the world. Black bass fishing in the Wallkill river, good drives and very healthy.

```
J. H. Decker, accommodates 20 ........... terms    $7 to  $10
J. A. Brewster, accommodates 15 .........     "      7 to   10
Mrs. J. R. Towlon, accommodates 10 ......     "      6 to   10
Occidental Hotel, accommodates 50 .......     "      6 to   10
Orange Hotel, accommodates 50 ...........     "      6 to   10
```

FLORIDA, ORANGE CO., N. Y.—5 miles from Goshen, among meadows and hills. Glenmere Lake, one of the handsomest lakes in the State, near by. Good fishing and hunting.

```
G. Seeley, accommodates 8 .............. terms    $6 to   $8
W. M. Sutton, accommodates 6 ...........     "      6 to    8
Mrs. Round, accommodates 6 .............     "      7 to    8
N. D. Houston, accommodates 10 ........      "      6 to    8
Bill House, accommodates 30 ............     "      6 to   10
```

MIDDLETOWN, ORANGE CO., N. Y.—67 miles from New York. Beautiful scenery, surrounding hills, woods and valleys. Fishing and boating in the Wallkill ; good woodcock and quail shooting.

Mrs. R. Boyd, accommodates 8	terms	$6 to	$10
W. C. Reeve, accommodates 6	"	6 to	8
R. C. Mead, accommodates 6	"	6 to	8
Mrs. C. S. Preston, accommodates 6	"	6 to	8
Mrs. G. Wood, accommodates 6	"	6 to	8
D. R. Miller, accommodates 8	"	6 to	8
Mrs. I. B. Toulon, accommodates 10	"	6 to	10
Mrs. L. F. Van Doren, accommodates 6	"	6 to	8
C. Z. Taylor, accommodates 3	"	6 to	8

OTISVILLE, ORANGE CO., N. Y.—76 miles from New York. A quiet farming neighborhood, in the midst of dairies, 1,200 feet above tide water. Woodcock and other game shooting in season.

S. Bertholf, accommodates 6	terms	$6
Mrs. M. O. Wilkin, accommodates 4	"	6
Mrs. M. J. Green, accommodates 4	"	8
Mrs J. H. Reed, accommodates 10	"	6
W. C. Tymerson, accommodates 20	"	6
Lemons' House, accommodates 20		6 to $40
Green's Hotel, accommodates 20		6 to 10

PORT JERVIS, ORANGE CO., N. Y.—87 miles from N. Y. Beautifully located on the Delaware and Neversink rivers, in the midst of fine scenery. Lakes and trout streams afford good fishing near by.

Delaware House, accommodates 50	terms	$8 to	$10
Union House, accommodates 20	"	8 to	10
H. Dutcher, accommodates 10	"		8

MILFORD, PIKE CO., PA.—7 miles from Port Jervis, situated on a high bluff overlooking the Delaware river, and surrounded by mountains. The center of a celebrated trout, bass, and pickerel fishing, and deer, bear, partridge, and woodcock region. There are no less than 100 falls in the vicinity, from 20 to 100 feet in height, and set in the midst of the wildest surroundings.

Maple Cottage, accommodates 25	terms	$10 to	$14
Cressman House, accommodates 120	"	10 to	14
Sawkill House, accommodates 100	"	10 to	12
River View House, accommodates 75	"		12
Bluff House, accommodates 100	"	10 to	15
Glen Cottage, accommodates 20	"	10 to	12
Barnes Cottage, accommodates 40	"	7 to	8
Miss F. Dimmicks, accommodates 50	"	10 to	14
Mr. De Behrls, accommodates 80	"	10 to	15
Fauchene House, accommodates 75	"	14 to	30
J. J. Ryman, accommodates 15	"	7 to	8
E. L. Van Eppen, accommodates 12	"	6 to	7

DINGMAN'S FERRY, PIKE CO., PA.—15 miles from Port Jervis. A resort in a part of the Delaware Valley, the character of whose surroundings have given it the name of the Switzerland of America. It is a region of cataracts, mountains, glens, gorges, and wonderful lakes.

Bellevue House, accommodates 50. A most delightful house surrounded with shady lawns. The table supplied with the best French cookery. Terms $8 to $14. Children and misses half price.

High Falls House, accommodates 150	terms	$10 to $14
Ran Van Corden's, accommodates 15	"	7 to 8

SHOHOLA, PIKE CO., PA.—107 miles from N. Y., on the banks of the Delaware, 1,000 feet above the sea. The best of hunting and fishing in season, among the grandest of mountain scenery. The post office address of the last two houses, is Eldred, Sullivan Co., N. Y.

Shohola House, accommodates 25	terms	$8
Isaac M. Bradley, accommodates 20	"	7
Mrs. J. A. Meyers, accommodates 30	"	8

LACKAWAXEN, PIKE CO., PA.—111 miles from N. Y., on the Delaware and Lackawaxen rivers, and in one of the finest hunting and fishing regions in the State. Surrounded by mountains, forests, streams, and lakes.

Delaware House, accommodates 100	terms	$8 to $12
Williamson House, accommodates 25	"	7
National Hotel, accommodates —	"	— to —
Vau Benschoten House, accommodates 15	"	6 to 10

BLOOMING GROVE, PIKE CO., PA.—Located among the mountains of Pike Co. Good hunting of all kinds. Large and small game. Reached by stage from Lackawaxen.

Blooming Grove Park House, accommodates 100	terms	$10 to $12
West Brook House, accommodates 15	"	6 to 10

HAWLEY, WAYNE CO., PA.—125 miles from N. Y. via. Honesdale branch from Lackawaxen, in the Pike Co. game and fish region. Splendid drives and one of the grandest excursion routes in the country.

Keystone House, accommodates 25	terms low.	
Eddy House, accommodates 6	"	$6
Wayne County House, accommodates 10	"	9

HONESDALE, WAYNE CO., PA.—135 miles from N. Y. via Honesdale branch from Lackawaxen; one of the handsomest villages in Pa., and at the head of the Delaware and Hudson Canal. Excellent drives, good hunting and fishing.

Allen House, accommodates 50	terms $6 to $10	
Kimble House, accommodates 10	"	5 to 6
Kiple House, accommodate s80	"	7 to 10

MONTICELLO, SULLIVAN CO., N. Y.—112 miles from N. Y., amid the most romantic scenery in the State, surrounded by lakes, trout streams and game preserves. Every variety of game can be found, deer, bear, foxes, partridge, quail, woodcock, English snipe, duck and wild pigeons in season. No malaria or fever. A mosquito was never seen in Monticello.

W. J. Lawson accommodates 25	terms	$4 to $	7
A. S. Landfield accommodates 30	"	7 to	10
Mrs. P. Brow, accommodates 18	"		7
Mrs. R. B. Towner, accommodates 30	"	8 to	10
D. L. Decker, accommodates 20	"	7 to	10
Mrs. M. A. Dougherty, accommodates 8	"	6 to	8
J. T. W. Coulter, accommodates 14	"	5 to	7
J. T. W. Mygatt, accommodates 10	"	6 to	7
Mrs. R. Tonner accommodates 30	"	8 to	10
L. A. Styls, accommodates 9	"		5
Mansion House, accommodates 80	"	7 to	10
Peter E. Palen, accommodates 12	"	7 to	15
J. J. Trowbridge, accommodates 12	"		6
Mrs. Elsie Krum, accommodates 10	"	5 to	7
N. L. Stern, accommodates 15	"	8 to	10
Mrs. Chas. Burnham, accommodates 15	"	16 to	20
W. H. & H. R. Reynolds, accommodates 20	"		5
John Hill, accommodates 15	"	5 to	7
Mrs. E. Toohey, accommodates 18	"		6
George Mapledoram, accommodates 8	"		5
George W. Decker, accommodates 20	"	6 to	8
A. D. Smith, accommodates 20	"		6
Mrs. H. Menzies, accommodates 12	"	6 to	8
George McLaughlin, accommodates 8	"	5 to	7

WHITE LAKE, SULLIVAN CO., N. Y.—Is located 8 miles south of Liberty Falls, and about ten miles west of Monticello, and has for many years been a favorite resort for sportsmen and their families. It derives its name from the whiteness of the sand on the shores and bottom, and the beautiful transparency of its waters. It is most conveniently reached by stage from Monticello Station, distant 9 miles.

Mansion House, accommodates 100	terms	$7 to	$10
Van Wert House, accommodates 75	"	7 to	10
Sunny Glade House, accommodates 40	"	8 to	10
J. H. Corby, accommodates 30	"	7 to	10
Mrs. S. B. Kirk, accommodates 30	"	8 to	10

NARROWSBURG, SULLIVAN CO., N. Y.—123 miles from N. Y., on the Delaware River. Mountain scenery, lakes and streams. Good fishing, and both large and small game for gunners.

Murray's House, accommodates 50	terms	$7 to	$12
Gibhard's Hotel accommodates 15	"		7
G. Ughling's Hotel, accommodates 20	"	—	—
John Engleman, accommodates 12	"		6
Willoughby Cottage, accommodates —	"		6

COCHECTON, SULLIVAN CO., N. Y.—129 miles from N. Y. A romantic location on the Delaware River, with lakes and streams around, and every attraction for sportsmen.

De Witt Knapp's Hotel, accommodates 15....terms		$6
John Barwig, accommodates 50...............	"	—
Leroy Bonesteil, accommodates 15	"	—
Temperance Hotel, accommodates 15........	"	—
Delaware House, accommodates 15	"	—
Peter Fahrenz, accommodates 20............	"	—

CALLICOON, SULLIVAN CO., N. Y.—136 miles from N. Y. Among wild and rugged scenery in the center of one of the most famous trout regions in the Delaware Valley.

Minard House, accommodates 30.............terms	$7 to	$8
Western Hotel, accommodates 40............	"	6 to	10
Callicoon Hotel, accommodates 20..........	"		5
Jacob Dietz, accommodates 15...............	"	5 to	7
M. H. Atwater, accommodates 10............	"	4 to	6

HANCOCK, DELAWARE CO., N. Y.—Situated 164 miles from N. Y., with an elevation of 1,005 feet. The east and west branches of the Delaware River are separated from each other by a lofty range of hills, the western face of which is very bold and precipitous. This mountain promontory comes to an abrupt and rocky point at Hancock, where the east and west branches unite to form the Delaware River.

Mrs. A. Hall, accommodates 25.............terms	$6 to	$8
Mr. A. Sheppard, accommodates 25..........	"	6 to	8
Hancock House, accommodates 50	"		5

NEWBURGH SHORT-CUT BRANCH.

This division of the Erie, which leaves the main line one mile east of Turner's, opens up a country that is wonderful in many ways.

CENTRAL VALLEY, ORANGE CO., N. Y.—49 miles from N. Y. Among mountains, lakes and streams. Good hunting and fishing, and perfectly healthy.

Summit Lake House, accommodates 50.......terms	—	—
Isaac L. Noxson, accommodates 35..........	"	$8 to	10
Mrs. E. Gibb, accommodates 10.............	"	7 to	9
G. R. Cory, accommodates 10	"	6 to	8
W. Hazard, accommodates 10...............	"	6 to	8
E. R. Mott, accommodates 10...............	"	6 to	8
David Connell, accommodates 30............	"	5 to	8
Henry Thorn Sir, accommodates 20	"	6 to	7
Col. A. H. Taylor, accommodates 15........	"	12 to	15
Samuel Polhamus, accommodates 15.........	"	7 to	10
G. T. Peckham, accommodates 20..........	"	8 to	10
E. Stockbridge, accommodates 80...........	"	6 to	12
C. T. Ford, accommodates 30...............	"	6 to	10

HIGHLAND MILLS, ORANGE CO., N. Y.—50 miles from N. Y.
Elevation, 1,200 feet above tide-water, on the shores of a lake.

Cromwell Lake House, accommodates 200	terms $7 to	$14
C. H. Townsend, accommodates 50	" 10 to	12
Jas. W. Campbell, accommodates 6	" 8 to	10
Charles Ford, accommodates 8	" 6 to	10

WOODBURY, ORANGE CO., N. Y.—51 miles from N. Y., in a quiet farming neighborhood, among mountain scenery, and contiguous to all the attractions of the region.

Misses J. and R. Hallock, accommodates 50	terms $8 to	$10
L. A. Van Clift, accommodates 30	" 8 to	10
Benj. Ford, accommodates 40	" 8 to	10
W. J. Cornell, accommodates 20	" 8 to	10
Lewis S. Joyce, accommodates 20	" 8 to	10
Benj. Hazard, accommodates 12	"	6
J. R. Hazard, accommodates 12	"	6

MOUNTAINVILLE, ORANGE CO., N. Y.—55 miles from New York, in a wild, deep gorge of the mountain, 1,500 feet above the plain. The views from this spot are grand.

John Orr, accommodates 40,	terms $7 to	$10
S. Shaw accommodates 25	" 7 to	10
S. Brundage, accommodates 30	" 7 to	10
S. E. Benjamin, accommodates 15	" 7 to	10
J. Bannell, accommodates 15	" 7 to	10
J. Mailler, accommodates 15	" 7 to	10
Mrs. C. C. Mailler, accommodates 30	" 7 to	10
N. Brundage, accommodates 20	" 6 to	9
J. W. Barton, accommodates 20	" 7 to	10
J. Q. Brown, accommodates 15	" 7 to	10
William Titus House, accommodates 40	" 7 to	10
S. Smith, accommodates 30	" 8 to	12
C. W. Tuthill, accommodates 25	" 7 to	10
H. W. Huise, accommodates 15	" 7 to	10
Capt. B. G. Handy, accommodates 35	" 6 to	9
Chas. Coleman, accommodates 15	" 7 to	10
A. Fredenburg, accommodates 15	" 6 to	9

CORNWALL, ORANGE CO., N. Y.—56 miles from New York. The fame of this resort is world-wide, no less than 5,000 people annually summer in this district. The town is built on a high elevation overlooking the river ; hotels are built on the very crest of the hills ; others overlook some yawning gorge or are almost hidden behind forest trees. The drives are unsurpassed, and the views of mountains, glens, streams, lakes and valleys, render it one of the most popular resorts in the country. Cornwall can also be reached by the steamer Mary Powell.

Elmer House, accommodates 250	terms $8 to	$15
Lawrence House, accommodates 100	" 8 to	10

River House, accommodates 60..............terms $8 to 12
Smith's House, accommodates 250............ " 8 to 15
Mountain House, accommodates 500.....terms $3.50 per day
Carswell House, accommodates 40..........terms $8 to $12
Turner House, accommodates 60............ " 8 to 12
Ducan House, accommodates 40............. " 8 to 12
Wiley House, accommodates 60............. " 8 to 12
Ryder House, accommodates 30............. " 8 to 12
Birdsall House, accommodates 50.......... " 8 to 12
Storm King House, accommodates 60........ " 8 to 10
Lebanon House, accommodates 30........... " 8 to 12
Brookside House, accommodates 40......... " 8 to 12
Wood House, accommodates 30.............. " 8 to 10
Vine Brook Cottage, accommodates 30...... " 8 to 10
Glen Ridge House, accommodates 350....... " 2 per day
Linden House, accommodates 200........... " 8 to 12
Willow Avenue House, accommodates 50.... " 8 to 10
Evergreen Lawn House, accommodates 60... " 8 to 10
Moodna House, accommodates 60........... " 8 to 12
Glen House, accommodates 30............. " 8 to 10
Ward House, accommodates 30............. " 3 per day
Highland House, accommodates 30......... " 3 "
Sagamore House, accommodates 40......... " 3 "
Union House, accommodates 30............ " 3 "
N. Chatfield, Jr., accommodates 15....... "
L. P. Clark, accommodates 40............ " 6 to $10
C. Birdsall, accommodates 50............ " 12
Willard Avenue House, accommodates 60... " 10 to 20

NEWBURGH, ORANGE CO., N. Y.—63 miles from New York, on the Newburgh Bay; celebrated for its Revolutionary associations, beautiful scenery and healthfulness.

H W. Murtfeldt, accommodates 35..........terms $6 to $8
Baldwin House, accommodates 150.......... " 8 to 12
Lake Side House, accommodates 60......... " 8 to 12
Highland Institute, accommodates 50....... " 8 to 12
Orange Hotel, accommodates 60........... " 8 to 12
Miss Vileys, accommodates 15............. " 7 to 10
United States Hotel, accommodates 125...... " 8 to 12

NEWBURGH BRANCH FROM GREY-COURT.

WASHINGTONVILLE, ORANGE CO., N. Y.—61 miles from New York, on the Newburgh Branch, and located in the celebrated dairy region of Orange Co.

Mrs. C. R. Ball, accommodates 8............terms   Apply
F. H. Keeler, accommodates 8............. " $7 to $8
D. S. Mead, accommodates 12............. " 7 to 8
A. H., Box 17, accomodates 30........... " 7 to 8

J. F. Murphy, accommodates 12..............terms $6 to   7
D. Goldsmith, accommodates 16..............   "   7 to   8
Miss M. Beatty, accommodates 20............   "   7 to   8
Mrs. A. E. Brooks, accommodates 20.........   "   6 to   8
T. B. Cameron, accommodates 20............   "   6 to   8

SALISBURY, ORANGE CO., N. Y.—64 miles from New York,
via the Newburgh Branch, in a pleasant and delightful
farming country; unsurpassed views and perfectly healthy.

R. W. Genung, accommodates 20.............terms $7 to $9
D. B. Howell, accommodates 20..............   "   7 to   9
J. Clemence, accommodates 20..............   "   7 to   9
A. Stewart, accommodates 30................   "   7 to   9
S. Moffatt, accommodates 10................   "   7 to   8
Mrs. R. Finley, accommodates 30............   "   7 to   9
Woangdale Villa, accommodates 14.........   "   8

HIGHLANDS OF CENTRAL NEW YORK,

ON THE LINE OF THE

New York, Ontario & Western R. R.

Reached *via* the New York, Lake Erie and Western Railway, or the New Jersey Midland Railway. Direct connections.

This region is unsurpassed in beauty and variety of landscape, with its mountain summits rising above 3,000 feet, and its narrow, but exquisitely lovely valleys, its numberless streams and waterfalls, its gem-like lakes, its rugged and gloomy hill sides, with their wealth of pines and hemlocks, its abundant game to attract the sportsmen, and its quiet nooks so grateful in the rest they offer to the weary brain, are now being appreciated by summer tourists.

The high elevation of this road, rising with the hills to nearly 2,000 feet above the sea, is a characteristic which especially commends it to summer tourists, for the bracing and health-imparting breezes which, even in the hottest days of summer, sweep over the hills.

BLOOMINGBURGH, SULLIVAN CO., N. Y.—It is 77½ miles from N. Y., with an elevation of 757 feet. It has a magnificent landscape of mountain, forest, lake and stream. The hunting and fishing are excellent.

William Andrews, accommodates 10	terms moderate.		
Mrs. E. A. Strong, accommodates 10	"	"	
Mrs. J. G. Gowley, accommodates 15	"	$6	
James Haire, accommodates 10	"	3 to	$7
Miss Emma Barrett, accommodates 30	"	6 to	7
E. Gardiner, accommodates 10	"	7	
Mrs. Lydia A. Waters, accommodates 30	"	5 to	7
W. H. Ellis, accommodates 20	"	6	

WURTSBORO, SULLIVAN CO., N.Y.—A neat and attractive village, 79 miles from New York, abounding with brooks and streams and beautiful lakes well stocked with trout, pickerel and black bass. Elevation, 720 feet.

The Guyman House, accommodates 50	terms $6 to	$7
Fred. Harding, accommodates 12	"	6

HOMOWACK, ULSTER CO., N. Y.—A delightful village, located on the Delaware and Hudson Canal. It is 86 miles from N. Y., with an elevation of 400 feet, and is at the junction of two pleasant valleys.

Homowack Hotel, accommodates 40 .... terms	$5	
John De Witt, accommodates 10 .... "	5	
Jas. W. Cudney, accommodates 15 .... "	6	
Sanford F. Cudney, accommodates 12 .... "	5	
J. B. Hauxhurst, accommodates 12 .... "	3 to	$6
Alvan Smith, accommodates 5 .... "	4	

ELLENVILLE, ULSTER CO., N. Y.—One of the most beautiful towns in the state, surrounded with many attractive points for sightseers, among which may be mentioned the Honk Falls, the Minnewaski Falls, and Ice Caves, where the ice has been preserved for ages.

Charles U. Whelpley, accommodates 10 .... terms	$5 to	$7
J. A. Meyers, accommodates 10 .... "	7 to	10
P. L. Garrison accommodates 50 .... "	7 to	8
Mrs. A. Baldwin, accommodates 15 .... "	moderate.	
Terwilliger House, accommodotes 20 .... "	$7 to $10	
J. F. Rheinhart, accommodates 10 .... "	7 to	10

SANDBURGH, SULLIVAN CO., N. Y.—A finely situated village on the Eastern slope of the Deleware Mountains. It is 962 feet above the sea and commands a fine view of forests, lakes, and valleys of the Neversink.

Elisha Stoddard, accommodates 20 .... mterms	$5 to	$6
Richard Hanyan, accommodates 10 .... "	5	

FALLSBURGH, SULLIVAN CO., N. Y.—Emerging from a tunnel of 650 feet through the mountains this beautiful village greets the eye. The elevation is 1,224 feet above the sea. It is here that the beautiful valley of the Neversink reaches its greatest grandure.

Peter Vandermark, accommodates 16 .... terms	$5 to	$8
John Gamble, accommodates 10 .... "	5	
N. Flagler, accommodates 35 .... "	6 to	10
A. H. Strong, accommodates 20 .... "	6 to	7

NEVERSINK, SULLIVAN CO., N. Y.—10 miles from Fallsburgh Station, amid rugged mountain scenery.

E. Vanderlyn, accommodates 15 .... terms	$4 to	$6
A. Herron, accommodates 65 .... "	7	

HURLEY, ULSTER CO., N. Y.—Located 100 miles from N. Y., with an elevation of 1,320 feet. The fishing and hunting facilities here are not surpassed anywhere in the State.

John Hogan, accommodates 20 .... terms	$6	
William Hogan, accommodates 20 .... "	$5 to 6	
P. G. Wright, accommodates 15 .... "	5 to 7	
Sineca Dutcher, accommodates 10 .... "	5 to 6	
Lewis Decker, accommodates 25 .... "	reasonable.	
Charles Rexford, accommodates 16 .... "	$5 to 7	
Garret Le Roy, accommodates 30 .... "	5	
A. B. Lavah, accommodates 10 .... "	5 to 6	

LIBERTY FALLS, SULLIVAN CO., N. Y.—Located 106 miles from N. Y., and 1,442 feet above the sea. At this point the railway crosses the valley of the east branch of the Mongaup River on a trestle 100 feet high and 1,100 feet long. The scenery is wild but grand.

T. W. Lane, accommodates 10	terms	$6
Thomas Keegan, accommodates 8	"	5
W. K. Leder, accommodates 20	"	5
John Maron, accommodates 12	"	5
A. Carrier, accommodates 10	"	5
John Monroe, accommodates 8	"	5
D. C. Palmer, accommodates 10	"	5

LIBERTY, SULLIVAN CO., N. Y.—Located 108 miles from N.Y., and 1,578 feet above the sea, yet in a valley surrounded by the towering summits of the Blue Mountains which rise a thousand feet above the village. The scenery is remarkable for its beauty, and the country around is the paradise of the amateur fisherman and sportsman.

Liberty House, accommodates 50	terms moderate.	
Col. A. J. Clements, accommodates 30	"	$6
George Gary, accommodates 20	"	6
William F. Sherwood, accommodates 10	"	6
Dr. Phebe Low, accommodates 5	"	5
B. C. Young, accommodates 30	"	8
John A. Shaw, accommodates 10	"	7
Mrs. A. Gildersleeve, accommodates 25	"	8
Charles Le Roy, accommodates 10	"	7
Nathan Harris, accommodates 20	"	7
Henry Le Roy, accommodates 25	"	8
Benjamin Willey, accommodates 30	"	8
Charles Gregory, accommodates 12	"	8
Joshua Geraw, accommodates 20	"	8
Peter Reddington, accommodates 10	"	7
Hugh Keenan, accommodates 7	"	7
J. B. Nichols, accommodates 35	"	$5 to 7
John Beck, accommodates 6	"	moderate.
John A. Darbee, accommodates 8	"	$8
Mrs. Iva P. Devine, accommodates 10	"	7
Victory Champlin, accommodates 25	"	8
John A. Clements, accommodates 20	"	7
Blake Gregory		
Thomas Guildersleeve, accommodates 10	"	7
Mrs. David Clements, accommodates 15	"	8
Abel Gregory	"	7
Flavius P. Carrier, accommodates 8	"	7
Mrs. Edwin Fobes, accommodates 10	"	9

COOKS FALLS, DELAWARE CO., N. Y.—Distance from N.Y. 130 miles. Elevation 1,184 feet. The post office address is Butternut Grove. This spot is another of those homes for sportsmen. A beautiful lake is near by.

Wallace Hill, accommodates 10	terms $5 50	
Mrs. Henry Pelham, accommodates 15	"	6

EAST BRANCH, DELAWARE CO., N. Y.—A well-known lumber station, convenient to Beaverkills and the East Branch of the Delaware River.

A. J. & D. C. Francisco, accommodates 25....terms $5 to $7

WALTON, DELAWARE CO., N. Y.—Located 168½ miles from N. Y., and 1,220 feet above the sea. The lofty range which forms the watershed between the Delaware and Susquehana Rivers rises on the northwest of the village, and at the north and northeast the western spurs of the Catskills reach an altitude of 3,000 feet.

Mrs. A. C. Seeley, accommodates 20 ....terms $4
Mrs. N. C. Morris, accommodates 12.............. "   6

DELHI, DELAWARE CO., N. Y.—Located 185 miles from N.Y., and 1,453 feet above the sea. The west branch of the Delaware passes to the west of this village. Surrounded on all sides by spurs of the Catskills which lose themselves in the most romantic valleys. One can drive in any direction and have at every step a shifting panorama of the wildest scenery.

W. H. Simmons, accommodates 12.........terms $8
D. W. Shaw, accommodates 16.... .... "   8
J. McMurray, accommodates 20.......... "   reasonable
B. Fitch, accommodates 12.... .... " $6

MEREDITH, DELAWARE CO., N. Y.—Located 6½ miles north of Delhi, at an elevation of 2,143 feet.

J. Albion Law, accommodates 20...........terms $7 to $10
J. B. McNaughton, accommodates 8..... ... "   4 to   6

MISCELLANEOUS RESORTS

— ON THE —

New York Central Railway, New Haven and Hartford Railway and others.

AVON SPRINGS, N. Y.—Delightfully situated on the Rochester division of the Erie railway, on the right bank of the Genesee River. The hotel accommodations are good.

Knickerbocker Hall..........................

Congress Hall ....

Avon Spring House ....

ARLINGTON, BENNINGTON CO., VT.—Rare mountainous scenery and health-giving air are the attractions. It is 200 miles from N. Y. and 8 miles from Manchester. Best route from N. Y. is via N. Y. C. R. R.

Arlington House, accommodates 20..........terms	$6 to	$12
Mrs. F. S. Canfield, accommodates 12...... "		6
N. H. Batchelder, accommodates 15 .... "	7 to	10
N. G. Hard, accommodates 15............... "	7 to	10

The post-office for the two last is East Arlington.

ADAMS STATION, ALBANY, CO., N. Y.—A pleasant and attractive village, located five miles from Albany. Reached from N. Y. via the N. Y. C. R. R.

Mrs. A. C. Roskerans, accommodates 10 ....terms	$6 to	$8
Mrs. Jane Flugler, accommodates 10 .... "	6 to	8
Mrs. De Groot, accommodates 10 .... "	6 to	8

BENNINGTON, VT.—

Mrs. Sarah Jewett, accommodates 10........terms	$10

BEDFORD, WESTCHESTER CO., N. Y.—39 miles from N. Y. via. Harlem R.R.; pleasantly located in a rich farming country.

Mrs. J. R. Jemmerson, accommodates 30......terms	$5 to $8

BRUSHTON, FRANKLIN CO., N. Y.—A pleasant and attractive farm country, with shaded walks, good drives and health-giving air. Reached via New York Central Railway.

Joseph Humphry, accommodates 20..........terms	$3 to	$5
Samuel E. Pease, accommodates 10.......... "		3
Mrs. J. H. Barnum, accommodates 5.......... "		3
Mrs. W. Conger, accommodates 8 .... "		

BRIDGEPORT, FAIRFIELD CO., CONN.—57 miles from N. Y. via New Haven Railway. Pleasantly located on the Sound. The bathing at this point is unusually fine as are also the drives.

Sterling House, accommodates 70 .... terms	$7 to	$10
Atlantic Hotel, accommodates 50 .... "	8 to	10
Golden Hill Hotel, accommodates 40 .... "	8 to	10

BARTON, ON THE SOUND, N. Y.—Delightfully located ; one mile from City Island ; a place surrounded by water and shade trees, and popular as a summer resort. Reached *via* New Haven Railroad.

J. Walton, accommodates 30 .... terms	$5 to	$10
Mrs. Stringham, accommodates 10 .... "	5 to	7
Charles Abbott, accommodates 10 .... "	5 to	7
Mrs. S. D. Hatton, accommodates 10 .... "	5 to	7
Mrs. Geo. Hallenbeck, accommodates 20 ..... "	4 to	7
Chas. McClensen, accommodates 20 .... "	4 to	7

BLOOMFIELD, ESSEX CO., N. J.—Reached in forty-five minutes *via* New York and Greenwood Lake R. R. This is a popular resort, and well patronized by summer boarders.

M. A. Meacham, accommodates 20 .... terms	$6 to	$8
J. W. Howell, accommodates 15 .... "	7 to	8
Mrs. W. P. Lyon, accommodates 20 .... "	6 to	8

CALDWELL, ESSEX CO., N. J.—17 miles from New York to Montclair station *via* Morris and Essex Railway, and from thence, a beautiful drive of 20 minutes to Caldwell. This is one of the healthiest places in the county, and offers many attractions to summer boarders.

A. A. Snyder, "Caldwell House." Grounds large and well shaded. Established 8 years . terms $5 to $10

CRARYVILLE, COLUMBIA CO., N. Y.—

Mrs. P. V. Snyder, accommodates 6 .... terms $5

CAPE MAY, N. J.—Distance from New York 141 miles, and reached *via* New Jersey Southern Railway. This celebrated beach is too well-known to require comment from us. The hotel accommodations cannot be surpassed. Among the principal hotels we will mention the :

Stockton House, accommodates 1200 . . terms	$3 to $4 per day
Congress Hall, accommodates 1000 ...., "	3 to 4 per day
National Hotel .... "	3 per day

A large number of smaller hotels and private boarding-houses who charge from $10 to $20 per week.

CAIRO, GREENE CO., N. Y.—10 miles from Catskill village, on high table land. Beautiful falls are in the hamlet, and the scenery is unsurpassed. Reached *via* the New York Central Railway.

Walters Bros., accommodates 50 .... terms	Apply.
Webster House, accommodates 30 .... "	"
Grand View House, accommodates 40 .... "	$7 to $10
Mrs. P. Raiders, accommodates 20 .... "	7 to 10

CATSKILL, GREENE CO., N. Y. Delightfully located on the banks of the Hudson. Elevation high, and mountain views unsurpassed. Reached by boat or N. Y. Central Railway.

Catskill Mountain House, accommodates 400, terms apply.		
Prospect Park House, accommodates 400	" $10 to	15
A. D. Wilbur, accommodates 8	" 6 to	10
Grant House, accommodates 300	" apply.	
Irving House, accommodates 75	" 8 to	10
Creek Side House, accommodates 75	" 8 to	10

CHATHAM, BARNSTABLE CO., MASS. Reached from N. Y., via New Haven R. R. A delightful town situated on the Elbo of Cape Cod, on the South Eastern extremity of Mass. A splendid Ocean view and plenty boating, fishing and gunning.

Ocean House, accommodates 25 terms	$6 to	$8
Eldridge House, accommodates 20 "	5 to	7
Watts House, accommodates 20 "	7 to	9
Geo. H. Howe, accommodates 15 "	7 to	9
T. O. Loveland, accommodates 15 "	7 to	9
Silas H. Harding, accommodates 6 "		6

CHATHAM, MORRIS CO., N. J. Located on the Delaware, Lackawanna and Western R. R. Time from N. Y., one hour.

Mrs. S. P. Purdy, accommodates 20 terms	$6 to	7
Mrs. J. Bayley, accommodates 15 "		6

DELAWARE WATER GAP, MONROE CO., PA. 92 miles from N. Y., via Morris and Essex Railway. It is at this point the Delaware River forces itself through the Blue Mountains. Elevation 1,600 feet.

Kittatinny House terms	$10 to	12
Water-Gap House "	12 to	20
Mountain House "	12 to	20

Good accommodations can be had in boarding-houses at from $9 to $12.

DURHAM, GREENE CO., N. Y. 20 miles from Catskill landing, high up in the mountains.

Shubal Finch, accommodates 20 terms	$6

DELAWARE STATION, WARREN CO., N. J.—75 miles from N. Y. and 7 miles from Delaware Water Gap, and ¼ mile from Delaware River. Fine mountain scenery, good fishing and hunting. Reached via Delaware, Lackawanna and Western Railway.

John Myers, accommodates 20 terms	$5 to	$7
Mrs. C. Coal, accommodates 6 "	5 to	6
Mrs. M. Bellis, accommodates 4 "		5
Mrs. M. Stiles, accommodates 10 "	5 to	7
Geo. W. Baird, accommodates 6 "	5 to	8
D. A. Ayers, accommodates 10 "	5 to	7

ENGLEWOOD, BERGEN CO., N. J.—Delightfully located on the Northern R. R. of N. J., about forty minutes out.

Englewood house, accommodates 70_____terms   Apply.
Palisade Mt. House_____ "   moderate.
Mrs. H. Rauls, accommodates 20_____ " $7 to $10

EAST ARLINGTON, BENNINGTON CO., VT.—8 hours from N. Y., via Harlem Extension Branch of the Central Vermont Railway. A pleasant rural location with a high elevation and pure bracing air.

N. H. Batchellor, accommodates 14_____terms $7

GREENWOOD LAKE, ORANGE CO., N Y.—50 miles from N. Y., via Montclair and Greenwood Lake R. R. This is a beautiful body of water 10 miles long, surrounded by rugged mountains.

Brandon House, accommodates 100_____terms $15
Lake Side House, accommodates 75 _____ '   15
Windimere House, accommodates 75_____ "   15

GUILFORD, NEW HAVEN CO., CONN.—90 miles from N. Y., via New Haven Railway, and delightfully located, convenient to the Sound.

Guilford Point House, accommodates 20____terms $10 to $15
Sachems Head House, accommodates 40_____ "   8

GREENWICH, FAIRFIELD CO., CONN.—28 miles from N. Y. via New Haven Railway. A finely located village, with well wooded surroundings, elevation high, overlooking the Sound.

Lenox House, accommodates 150 _____terms $10 to $15
Holley Farm, accommodates 40_____ "   8 to 12
Rev. S. Howland, accommodates 10_____ "   8 to 10
Mrs. J. Finels, accommodates 15_____ "   10

HACKENSACK, BERGEN CO., N. J.,—40 minutes from N. Y., via The New Jersey and New York R. R. A well-known and popular place for summer residence.

G. Records, accommodates 6_____terms $6
Mrs. J. Terhune, accommodates 20_____ "   5 to 7
M. Y. Bunn, accommodates 15_____ "   7
Mansion House, apply for particulars_____

KATONAH, WESTCHESTER CO., N. Y.—42 miles from N. Y., via the Harlem R.R. A pleasant place, having many attractions for summer boarders.

Joseph D. Burt, accommodates 15_____terms $6 to $8
Avery House, accommodates 40_____ "   8 to 10
Abram Merritt, accommodates 30____ _____ "   7 to 10

MONTCLAIR, ESSEX CO., N. J.—Reached in 40 minutes from N. Y., via Montclair & Greenwood Lake R. R. A popular town for summer residence.

Walnut Mansion, accommodates 100_____terms $7 to $10
Ashland Hall, accommodates 30_____ "   6 to 10

MILFORD, NEW HAVEN CO., CONN.—63 miles from N. Y., via New Haven Railroad. Situated among shadowy elms and green hills.

Mrs. C. Merwin, accommodates 12..........terms $6 to $10
Milford House, accommodates 20.......... "   8 to 10
Sea Side House, accommodates 20....... "   10 to 15
Meadows End House..................Apply for particulars.

NEW ROCHELLE, WESTCHESTER CO., N.Y.—17 miles from N. Y., via New Haven Railway, and pleasantly located in close proximity to the Sound.

Leroy House, accommodates 40............terms $8 to $10
Premium Point House................apply for particulars.
Mrs. J. B. Kellogg, accommodates 15.......terms $8 to $12

NEW LONDON, NEW LONDON CO., CONN.—124 miles from New York, on the west bank of the river Thames, and con venient to the Sound. The harbor at this point is one of the best in the country. Reached via New Haven Railway or boat.

Crocked House, accommodates 200.........Apply for terms.
Metropolitan Hotel, accommodates 70.......terms $7 to $14
Pequot House, accommodates 500.......... " $5 per day.

NEW MILFORD, LITCHFIELD CO., CONN.—35 miles from Bridgeport, among the never ending attractions of the Housatonic Valley. Reached via New Haven Railway.

Fort Hill Mt. House, accommodates 40.....terms Moderate.
E. A. Thayer, accommodates 20............ "   "
Mrs. B. Treat, accommodates 15........ ... " $8
E. T. Brewer, accommodates 15............ " $7 to 10

NORWALK, FAIRFIELD CO., CONN.—43 miles from N. Y. One of the most popular resorts in the State. Excellent harbor, good boating, bathing and fishing. Reached via New Haven Railway.

Mrs. J. F. Raymond, accommodates 20 ......terms $6 to $7
Mrs. G. Ryder, accommodates 12............ "   7 to 8
Mrs. A. Comstock, accommodates 15......... "   7
The Allin and Lucas are the popular hotels at South Norwalk.

NYACK, ROCKLAND CO., N. Y.—Pleasantly located on the Hudson, almost opposite Tarrytown, and connected with it by a steam ferry. Nyack is a popular summer resort. It is most conveniently reached via Northern R. R. of New Jersey.

Prospect House, accommodates 20..........Apply for terms.
Smithsonian Hotel, accommodates 30 .... "   "
The Palmer House, overlooking village and
river. Mrs. M. E. English, accommodates 30,   terms $5 to $6

NARRAGANSETT PIER, WASHINGTON CO., R. I.—May be reached by the New Haven Railway or by Fall River steamboats. It is located at the mouth of Narragansett Bay, and has been a celebrated resort for years. The surf is light, and the boating and fishing excellent.

Tower Hill House	$4 per day.
Atwood House	terms $12 to $18
Continental Hotel	" 12 to 18
Delevan House	" 12 to 18
Atlantic Hotel	" 12 to 18
Narragansett Hotel	" 12 to 18
Ocean House	" 12 to 18
Sea View House	" 12 to 18
Mount Hope House	" 12 to 18

PEEKSKILL, WESTCHESTER CO., N. Y.—42 miles from New York via New York Central Railway. A pleasant place of summer residences, located directly on the Hudson River.

Elijah Tompkins, accommodates 20 ....terms $6
W. R. Jones, accommodates 10 ....   "   7

PELHAM, WESTCHESTER CO., N. Y.—33 minutes by rail from the Grand Central Depot, 42d street. The proximity of this place to New York serves to make it a charming spot for summer residence. Reached by the New Haven Railroad.

Mrs. M. A. Wood, accommodates 30 ....terms $6 to $8
This is a private residence, known as the Osborn House, with large and attractive grounds.

PINE BUSH, ORANGE CO., N. Y.—60 miles from N. Y., via New York, Ontario and Western Railway. High, healthy location.
Mrs. N. Keesler, accommodates 10 ....terms $7

POMFRET, WINDHAM CO., CONN.
Capt. Erastus Blackman, accommodates 12...terms $5 to $8

PORT EWEN, ULSTER CO., N. Y.—90 miles from N. Y., and only five minutes ride from Rondout, and close by the Hudson River.
Mrs. C. Tremper, accommodates 12............terms $5 to $6

RICHFIELD SPRINGS, OTSEGO CO., N. Y.—Reached via the Delaware, Lackawanna and Western R. R. There are seventeen springs near the village, which are considered especially efficacious in diseases, of the skin.

American Hotel, accommodates 400.........terms $10 to $12
Spring House, accommodates 500...........   "   15 to   20
National Hotel, accommodates 200...........   "   10 to   15
Central Hotel, accommodates 75..............   "   8 to   10
J. B. Cushman, accommodates 20...........   "   8 to   10

RYE, WESTCHESTER CO., N. Y.—27 miles from N. Y., via New Haven Railway. Located in close proximity to the Sound. The village is pretty and the drives in the vicinity are delightful.

Rye Beach Hotel, accommodates 75...........terms $8 to $12
Cliff House, accommodates 50..............   "   8 to   12
Mrs. F. Nicholas, accommodates 15 ....   "   7 to   8

SARATOGA SPRINGS, SARATOGA CO., N. Y.—182 miles from N. Y. via N. Y. Central R. R. This is one of the most famous summer resorts in the United States. Its mineral springs are of the highest order; its lakes, drives, and old elms form but a part of the many attractions here to be met with. 30,000 to 40,000 visitors may be found here at almost any time during August and September.

Congress Hall can accommodate 1200..terms per day		$3 to $5
Grand Union, can accommodate 1800..	"	"	3 to 5
United States, can accommodate 2,100..	"	"	3 to 5
Clarendon, can accommodate 500......	"	"	4
Windsor, can accommodate 500........	"	"	4
Warren, can accommodate 250,........	"	"	3 to 4
American, can accommodate 450.......	"	"	3 to 4
Everett, can accommodate 200........	"	"	3 to 4

Many smaller hotels may be found, also a large number of boarding-houses.

SCHROON LAKE, ESSEX CO., N. Y.—Reached via N. Y. C. R. R. from N. Y. One of the most delightful sections amid the Adirondack Mountains. The lake is 10 miles long and 2½ wide, with beautiful surroundings, The boating and fishing on the lake is unsurpassed.

Leland House.........................terms $10 to $15
Schroon Lake House...............	"	10 to 12
Ondawa House....................	"	10 to 12
Windsor House...................	"	8 to 10
J. B. Taylor, can accommodate 25..........	"	7 to 8

SILVER LAKE, ESSEX CO., N. J.—11 miles from N. Y., via Morris and Essex Railway. Time, 25 minutes. Also short distance from Bloomfield. Elevation high and healthy. Delightful lake near the house. Direct letters to Bloomfield.

Mrs. H. S. Britton, accommodates 20.......terms $6 to $10

SOUTH DURHAM, GREEN CO., N. Y.—Delightfully located in the Catskill Mountains, 15 miles from Catskill landing and 7 miles from South Caro.

J. V. Hulse of the Hulse's Mountain Retreat House, accommodates 40 to 50.............terms $7 to $8

SPRING VALLEY, ROCKLAND CO., N. Y.—30 miles from N. Y. via New Jersey and New York R. R.; a popular summer resort for many city boarders.

Glen House, accommodates 40................terms $6 to $8
T. Lockwood, accommodates 10..............	"	5 to 8
B. Barnard, accommodates 30...............	"	5 to 7

SCHOOLEY'S MOUNTAIN, MORRIS CO., N. J.—This favorite resort lies among the Highlands of New Jersey, and is reached either by the Morris & Essex R. R. from Hacketts-town, or Central of New Jersey from German Valley Station. Good hunting and fishing.

Heath House, accommodates 400...........terms $14 to $18
Belmont Hall, accommodates 250........... " 12 to 16

STRATFORD, FAIRFIELD CO., CONN.—60 miles from N. Y.
via New Haven Railway. Delightfully located on the banks
of the Housatonic River among overhanging elms.

S. W. Benjamin, accommodates 25.........terms
Mr. Geo. Fryer, accommodates 12............ " $6 to $8
Freeman Curtis, accommodates 20............ " 6 to 8

SING SING, WESTCHESTER CO., N. Y.—33 miles from N. Y.
via New York Central Railway, situated on the east bank
of the Hudson River.

J. B. Van Houton, accommodates 10..........terms $7 to $8
Mrs. C. Gilbert, accommodates 20............ " 6 to 8
Mrs. Rutherford, accommodates 15............ " 6 to 8
S. H. Beatty, accommodates 20............... " 7 to 8
J. B. Orsee, accommodates 15................ " 6 to 8

TARRYTOWN, WESTCHESTER CO., N. Y.—29 miles from
N. Y. via New York Central Railway, situated on a high
elevation commanding a fine view of the Hudson River.

Cliff House, accommodates 100...............terms $7 to $8
Irving House, accommodates 40.............. " 8 to 12
H. A. Kintzler, accommodates 15........... " 5 to 7
Mrs. Blakeman, accommodates 15............ " 6 to 7

WAWARSING, ULSTER CO., N. Y.—7 miles from Ellenville
Station on the Ontario and Western Railway. Free conveyance to house. Elevation high. Good trout fishing,
hunting, and perfectly healthy.

Edgar Vernovy, accommodates 16......... ......terms $6

WEST BRIGHTON, RICHMOND CO., STATEN ISLAND.—
45 minutes from N. Y., via Staten Island Ferry. House
convenient to landing, on a high terrace overlooking the Bay.
Fine boating, bathing, and fishing. Photograph may be
seen at the office of the American Summer Resort Directory,
5 Murray street.

Miss Willicse Cuthbert, accommodates — .... $8 to $12

WOODBOURNE, SULLIVAN CO., N. Y.—4 miles from Fallsburgh, (see page 51). Large roomy house on a farm of 240
acres, among hills and forests.

John Murphy, accommodates 30..............terms $5 to $9

NOTE.

Information concerning all

COUNTRY BOARDING PLACES

May be had at the Publication Office
of the

American Summer Resort Directory.

Full particulars in detail will be furnished concerning many select houses,
for whom we act as agents.

ALLEN & CO.,

5 MURRAY STREET

PUBLISHERS.

ALLEN & CO.,

REAL ESTATE

——AND——

COMMISSION BROKERS,

OFFICE:

5 MURRAY STREET, N. Y. CITY.

Give special attention to the sale of

COUNTRY PROPERTY.

Parties having improved or unimproved **REAL ESTATE** to sell, should send full particulars at once.

Those wishing to purchase can always find a good selection at their office.

They guarantee satisfaction to all parties.

They take full charge of Estates, Collections, Repairs, Improving or Building.

ESTABLISHED 1866.

www.ingramcontent.com/pod-product-compliance
Lightning Source LLC
Chambersburg PA
CBHW020243090426
42735CB00010B/1814